Phuket

Front cover: Hat Kata Noi

Right: orchids are common in Phuket

Hat Patong Phuket's most popular beach is the place to go for all manner of water sports (page 28)

The Similan Islands Explore the waters of these uninhabited islands, rated among the world's top ten dive sites (page 73)

Khao Phra Taew National Park Waterfalls, rare flowers and gibbons make trekking here a magical experience (page 57)

Island-hopping Choose a tropical paradise to the east of Phuket (page 66)

Promthep Cape Arrive early if you want a good spot for the spectacular sunsets (page 64)

Phang Nga Bay Take a cruise around this bizarre seascape, scattered with towering limestone pillars (page 70)

Tui Tui temple This old Chinese temple is the main focus of Phuket's annual Vegetarian Festival (page 49)

Phuket Town Take a walking tour around the colonial mansions and Sino-Portuguese shop-houses (page 45)

Siam Niramit See dramatic stage shows highlighting Thai culture (page 52)

Ko Phi Phi This is all you'd want of an island paradise (page 77)

A PERFECT TOUR

Day 1–2 — Relaxing spa

Beat the jetlag with an overnight stay in the northwest of the island at one of Phuket's luxury spas, such as the JW Marriott or Laguna Phuket. Pampering treatments will include a Thai massage, which is based on techniques believed to have been devised by the Buddha's personal physician over 2,000 years ago.

Day 5–6 — Eerie lagoons

Book a kayak tour in Phuket Town to explore Phang Nga Bay, where strange rock formations jut from the sea, and grab a photo in front of James Bond Island. At night camp out under a star-filled sky.

Day 7 — Phuket Town

Stroll the tiny streets of Phuket Town, which was the centre of the 19th-century tin-mining that brought Chinese workers and traders to the island. Many of the old shop-houses and mansions are now museums, cafés or galleries. Later explore the shopping at EXPO Market or Talad Tai Rot.

Day 3–4 — Take to the beach

Spend the days on Hat Patong, Phuket's most raucous beach, where you can watch the banana boats, parasailing and jet-skis in action. If you want some peace, take a boat to Freedom Beach just around the bay. At night catch a Thai boxing match before heading to Patong's notorious clubs and bars.

OF PHUKET

Day 9–11 Dive, dive, dive

Take a scuba course at Kata Beach, then head out to the open seas on a live-aboard boat. Within easy reach are dive sites like Ko Racha, Shark Point and the Similan Islands, where you can check out the coral, and search for leopard sharks, manta rays and turtles. Sleep overnight with uninhabited shores as your backdrop.

Day 13–14 Ko Phi Phi

Take a speedboat from Rawai to Ko Phi Phi for snorkelling, photo-ops with monkeys, and the beautiful Maya Bay, the location for many scenes in the movie *The Beach*. Look out for ancient wall paintings at the Viking Cave, and there's still time for a final beach party.

Day 8 Kata

Enrol on a cooking course at the famous Boathouse restaurant in Kata, followed by a waterfront lunch. Then take in the views as you climb Kata Hill for trekking at the Kok Chang Elephant Camp.

Day 12 Culture fix

Learn about the Heroines' Monument at Thalang Museum, before heading for Khao Phra Taew National Park, to visit the Gibbon Rehabilitation Centre and picnic by a waterfall. The adventurous can try cable skis in Kathu.

LOBSTER
220 ฿ / 100 GM.

CONTENTS

INTRODUCTION

Phuket (pronounced 'poo-get') is marketed as the 'Pearl of the Andaman', reflecting its shape as well as its physical beauty. At around 540 sq km (210 sq miles), it is Thailand's largest island. As a province, including nearby islands, it is Thailand's smallest and its second richest after Bangkok. It has been transformed over the past three decades from a sleepy little island into the country's most popular beach destination, receiving an escalating volume of visitors, currently standing at around 4.5 million each year. Its sandy white beaches and crystal waters also lure an increasing number to emigrate here.

Phuket's interior is mountainous, with the highest peak reaching 529m (1,735ft). Roads link the main points of interest, and although the areas surrounding the beaches are flat and easy to navigate on foot, the sheer size of the island makes transport a necessity if you intend to explore it fully. Striking headlands of varying height and length punctuate the 48km (30-mile) shoreline that runs down the west coast. It is here that you will find the majority of accommodation, sights and attractions. Phuket's beaches each have a unique appeal, and range from tiny, rarely visited coves whose waters teem with tropical fish, to bustling hives of action where beach activities and large numbers of people are the norm.

There are few beaches on the largely undeveloped east coast; instead this area is a haven for sailors. Yachts regularly sail around the tranquil Laem Pan Wa peninsula, or set sail from Laem Pan Wa towards the neighbouring province of Phang Nga to the north, where hundreds of pinnacles jut from perfectly still seawaters.

One of Phuket's beautiful beaches

Hat Nai Harn

Dry and wet seasons

Phuket has two distinct seasons – dry and wet. The dry season begins in November, when skies are blue, clouds are largely absent and humidity is low. Temperatures hover around the low to mid 30s (86–95°F). March and April are still within the dry season, but both heat and humidity begin to rise in preparation for the wet season. Temperatures regularly reach the high 30s (100°F), and occasionally even creep into the 40s (110°F). Sea breezes provide relief, and virtually all buildings are air conditioned, but it is still extremely hot. Without adequate sun protection, it can take as little as five minutes for skin to burn.

By May, temperatures begin to drop as the monsoon winds and rains cool the island. The rains usually last until around November. Despite the occasional extended rainy spell, however, storms often blow in only during the late afternoons and evenings. Large periods of the 'wet' season have been known to see no rain at all. Daytime temperatures between May and November are pleasant, usually hovering around the mid to high 20s (77–84°F).

Phuket's peak season is, predictably, in the middle of the dry season, which coincides with Christmas and the New Year. The island is always at maximum capacity at this time, and it is advisable to book accommodation well in advance.

Flora and fauna

Warm temperatures and jungle-filled interiors provide perfect conditions for a wide range of flora and fauna. Towering palm trees grow island-wide, and deep-purple orchids are in such abundance that they frequently appear as decorations in drinks, on hotel-room pillows and threaded together as flower garlands for sale on the streets and in bars. Orchid farms dotted across Phuket sell flowers to take home, and have demonstrations showing how to cultivate them.

As little as 100 years ago, a missionary named John Carrington reported seeing tigers and elephants roaming the island. Wild tigers are a thing of the past, but there are still large numbers of elephants on Phuket – although they can now be seen only inside the island's well-maintained elephant camps. Phuket's forested interiors are still home to a few species of wild monkeys, along with many birds and reptiles.

The Orchid Garden in Phuket Town

There are over 40 varieties of snake on the island, of which several are poisonous. The most dangerous are those from the pit-viper

Wat Chalong

family and the notorious cobra, but snakebites are extremely rare. Snakes typically avoid populated areas, but common sense dictates that any seen should be presumed poisonous and avoided. Far more common are geckos and other small lizards, which appear mainly after dark and gather in groups around lights and neon signs in a search of an insect dinner.

Religious beliefs on Phuket

The island has a permanent population of about 350,000, of whom the majority are Theravada Buddhists. Interestingly, Phuket has more mosques than Buddhist *wats* (temples), although with their grand designs and central positioning (so more often visited by the island's guests), temples give the appearance of being greater in number. Around 35 percent of the island's inhabitants are Muslim. It should be noted that the violence in the nearby south of Thailand has not spread to Phuket, and there is little or no religious tension between Phuket's Buddhists and Muslims. Many people of Chinese descent on the island practise Taoism, which is the inspiration for Phuket's famous Vegetarian Festival *(see page 49)*.

Although smaller in number, other faiths, including Christianity and Sikhism, are also recognised and readily accepted. Visitors to temples are expected to dress modestly in clothing that covers the knees and shoulders. Shoes, hats and sunglasses should be removed before entering. Some mosques allow foreign visitors, but not when ceremonies are taking place. There are a number of Christian churches across the island, and all welcome international visitors.

Tourism in paradise

By both Thai and international standards, Phuket is a very rich island. There was a time when most of the island's revenue was earned from tin mining, but when tin prices began to fall, many local landowners sold their land to eager developers, making big profits in the process. Phuket emerged as a tourist destination from the late 1970s onwards, and tourism remains the leading source of income today. There are, however, a number of local residents who still maintain a more traditional lifestyle, working in the rubber and pineapple plantations.

Although mainly a beach resort, Phuket has orchid farms, forests and wild parks. Phuket Town's centre is a mixture of quaint and modern shops, newly emerging department stores, local markets and grand colonial buildings. There are viewpoints, sunset spots and temples galore, and visitors can enjoy scuba diving, snorkelling, yachting, water-skiing, windsurfing, jet-skiing and parasailing. Boat trips on longtails, yachts, speedboats and Chinese junks run daily.

Nightlife is plentiful. Phuket Town boasts a number of entertainment establishments, and the famous

The Buddhist year

To calculate the year according to the Thai calendar, which is based on the death of Buddha, add 543 to the current international year. Songkran (Thai New Year) is in April, but the year changes on 1 January to make international business easier.

A Muslim girl in Ko Lanta

Soi Bangla in Patong has clubs, pubs and bars on a scale that cannot be matched elsewhere. At the other end of the spectrum, there are intimate beach bars, hilltop jazz bars and romantic restaurants.

Activities range from jungle walks and elephant treks to bungee jumping and horse riding. Golfers are spoilt for choice, with several fine courses and a number of smaller greens and driving ranges. Spas, massage outlets and beauticians around the island are ready and willing to pamper. There are large shopping centres, department stores, art and antique galleries and markets.

Coping with popularity

One downside to Phuket's continuing popularity is its shrinking capacity to handle what may now be perceived as overload. Emerging tourism markets, notably Russian and Chinese, pushed airport arrivals and departures past the unprecedented 8 million mark in 2011. To deal with the long airport queues, inevitably, development continues apace. More hotels, shops, cars and visitor attractions continue to place pressure on Phuket's natural resources – the very springs of its popularity – and commentators are now talking of the dangers of Phuket becoming an island city that feeds neighbouring attractions such as Krabi and Phang Nga. Care will be needed in the coming years to maintain the allure of the Pearl of the Andaman.

A BRIEF HISTORY

Throughout the ages, Phuket has held a magnetic appeal for those who stumbled across its shores. The first inhabitants are thought to have arrived about 40,000 years ago. These hunter-gatherers inhabited an island that was almost completely covered in rainforest. They were joined in the 1st century BC by Indian settlers. The first written mention of the island was in the 2nd century AD, in the work of Claudius Ptolemy, a Greek geographer and astronomer, who published a map showing what seems to be Phuket. Early maps of Thailand (known as Siam until the early 20th century) refer to Phuket as Jang Si Lang, which was translated into English as Junk Ceylon.

An early map of Thailand

Phuket's deposits of tin attracted attention from very early times. Although no written records accurately date the initial discovery of tin, analysis of cave drawings and other artefacts suggests that it could date back as far as the Stone Age. In ancient times, rain would wash away soil to expose the underlying tin, allowing people access to it. Tin mining began much later.

Sea gypsies (*chao lay*) were early coastal inhabitants of Phuket. They still live in small numbers in coastal communities around the island, leading a simple, mainly self-sufficient lifestyle, unlike their forebears in previous centuries, who made a living from piracy and pearl-fishing.

Phuket's early history

Little is known of Phuket's history until the 16th century, when European traders first became interested in the possibilities of the island's tin deposits. Later, in the 17th and 18th centuries, European sea captains took advantage of Phuket's geographical position along the maritime trading routes between China and India. They recognised the island as a source of fresh water and firewood, and many ships would anchor in the island's bays and coves, replenishing their provisions and waiting in safety for days, weeks or even months for the northeast monsoon winds to cease before continuing safely on their passage.

Invasion by the Burmese

In 1785 Phuket came under siege during an attempted invasion by the Burmese army. Sir Francis Light, a former British East India Company captain, who had moved to the island

Phuket almost becomes British

When the British secured a tin-mining concession in the mid-1770s, they considered Phuket as a possible base for controlling the Malacca Straits. They sent a British East India Company captain, Sir Francis Light, to reconnoitre the island, and came close to claiming Phuket as part of the British Empire. Ultimately, however, Britain opted for Penang in Malaysia instead. Captain Light fell in love and married a local island girl. His relocation to Phuket would prove significant in years to come, when he tipped off Phuket's administration that the Burmese army was going to invade the island.

Burmese ship in a battle against the Thais

years previously and married a local girl, witnessed the Burmese forces preparing to attack and sent word to Phuket's administration warning them of the threat. A defence was mounted by Lady Chan, the wife of Phuket's recently deceased governor, and her sister Lady Mook, who rallied the people and rapidly put forces in position to defend the island. For a month the Burmese attacked Phuket, trying to overrun it as part of a wider strategy to invade Thailand, but on 13 March they were forced to abort their invasion. The two sisters were credited with the successful defence of Phuket, and were awarded the honorary titles of Thao Thep Kasatri and Thao Sri Sunthon by Siam's King Rama I. Statues of the two sisters with swords drawn stand today on top of the Heroines' Monument in the Thalang district *(see page 56)*.

Burmese forces invaded again during the reign of King Rama II (1809–24); this time they were successful. Islanders were forced to flee to the neighbouring province of Phang

Lady Chan and Lady Mook, defenders of Phuket

Nga until the Burmese threat subsided. They returned to the northern part of Phuket and founded the town of New Thalang (since renamed Thalang), midway between where Phuket International Airport and Phuket Town now stand. Thalang was prominent until the discovery of tin in the south demanded an administrative location closer to the centre of the industry. Tongkah, now a district of Phuket Town, was formed.

The tin-mining era

The settlement became the administrative centre of the southern provinces of Siam, where tin production, now dominated by the Chinese, was the main source of revenue. Tongkah was officially elevated to the status of a town in 1850. As Phuket's economy boomed, the demand for workers rose, and Chinese immigrants arrived in larger numbers to work in the mines, mainly from the region's major port, Penang, to where most of the tin was also shipped. Today these early trade links still mark the ethnic character of Phuket, which has the highest percentage of ethnic Chinese in Thailand.

The Miners' Rebellion

The good fortune brought to Phuket by the economic success of the tin-mining industry was not without its problems. In 1876, rivalries between two Chinese secret societies, coupled with the miners' dissatisfaction with working conditions, led to the Miners' Rebellion. Miners and police faced off in vicious battles that spilled onto the streets, until Luang Pro Chaem, a prominent monk, eventually calmed the crowds and healed the rift by acting as a mediator between the opposing parties. Luang Pro Chaem set and healed many of the broken bones and wounds that resulted from the battles. A statue paying tribute to him and the good deeds he did for the people of Phuket can be seen at the famous Wat Chalong temple.

The colonial period

As the economy prospered, some of the Chinese immigrants became wealthy mine-owners. During the 19th century, the face of Phuket Town steadily began to change, to reflect the culture of the now dominant Chinese and the influence of Europeans. Grand mansions and shop-houses were built in the distinctive Sino-Portuguese style *(see page 45)*, which the Chinese borrowed from British colonies in Singapore and what is now Malaysia, where buildings were in turn influenced by Portuguese architecture in Malacca. Many of these buildings still stand today in the older quarters of Phuket Town, having been renovated and transformed into cafés, art galleries and museums.

Colonial buildings, Phuket Town

浩氣

The rubber industry

Henry Nicholas Ridley, a botanist at the Singapore Botanical Garden, discovered the full potential of the rubber tree in 1888 when he devised a way to propagate the trees swiftly and tap them for their sap, using an environmentally friendly method that is essentially the same today. A small cup collects the latex flowing from a short downward spiral cut into the tree's bark each night, but stretching only up to one-half of the tree's circumference. The cool night air allows the latex to flow before it coagulates in the daytime heat, sealing the cut. Later, the other side of the tree is cut, allowing the first wound to heal.

Rubber-tapping

Phuket's first rubber tree arrived in the early 20th century, and soon the trees began appearing in straight lines across the landscape – more than one-third of the island is now covered with plantations. As with the tin-mining industry, rubber-tapping called for a new wave of immigrants to meet the rising workload. This time it was not the Chinese, but Muslims from what is now Malaysia who arrived in droves. Thai Muslims still account for the majority of those working in Phuket's rubber plantations.

Rubber export was extremely lucrative, but over the years demand for natural latex went through a series of ups and downs. Aircraft and automobile manufacturers required rubber in large quantities to make tyres, but when the cost of synthetic rubber came down after the 1940s, the demand for natural latex decreased. The industry spiralled downwards and many rubber plantations were abandoned. However, the mid-1980s saw a dramatic and sudden turnaround when the worldwide Aids epidemic

Diving is big business in Phuket

created a huge demand for natural latex to manufacture condoms and surgical gloves. Most of Phuket's rubber plantations were gradually brought back into production and are once again busy. They are continually being upgraded with higher-yielding trees.

The modernisation of Phuket

At the beginning of the 20th century, a huge fire ravaged most of the downtown area of Phuket Town. The town was subsequently rebuilt, with new roads, public buildings and improved canals, and more traders began to settle with their families into what was becoming a relatively modern city. Governor Rassada Korsimbi led the reconstruction effort. Rassada Road was named in his honour.

Tourism came to the island in the 1970s, when the rubber industry was in a slump and there were no more profits to be made from tin mining. But there were formidable obstacles to be overcome before mass tourism could become

Phuket for sports

Sports enthusiasts have been among the main beneficiaries of Phuket's tourism boom since the 1970s. Along with world-famous diving tours have come sports like para-gliding, cable skiing and big game fishing. Events such as The King's Cup regatta (www.kingscup.com) and the Phuket Triathlon (www.lagunaphukettriathlon.com) now draw competitors from around the globe.

viable. Despite its relatively large size, Phuket was at that time fairly isolated. The few roads were primitive, and during the monsoon season virtually impassable. The only way to reach Phuket was by boat until Phuket International Airport was constructed in 1972. At the same time, a major road-building project commenced, and the first tourist accommodation appeared in the form of a few basic bungalows on Patong Beach, which at the time was all but deserted. Backpackers were the first to discover the island's pristine beaches.

Phuket experienced an almost overnight transition from an industrial- to a tourism-driven economy. The island's popularity among foreign visitors skyrocketed, and in the 1980s and 1990s Phuket saw a spurt of resort-building to cope with the demand. The new millennium, however, brought with it many challenges. In 2002, Sudden Acute Respiratory Syndrome (Sars) spread throughout Asia, threatening to affect the tourism industry, as did the Avian flu epidemic the following year.

But catastrophe struck in 2004. The deadly tsunami that invaded Phuket's shores on 26 December was triggered by an undersea earthquake in the Indian Ocean off the west coast of Sumatra. A series of enormous waves crashed onto Thailand's western coast over the coming hours, causing an official death toll of 5,395, with a further 2,845 listed as missing.

Tsunami memorial lanterns

On Phuket alone, an estimated 320 people were killed, although unofficially many more are thought to have died because of the vast numbers of illegal workers on the island (many of them from Burma). Kamala was one of the worst-hit beaches, but Patong was also very badly affected. Tributes to the dead are held annually across the island, and life-saving measures have been put into place in case another tsunami occurs. Warning towers are positioned along all beaches to sound the alarm, and signs show the way to safe evacuation areas inland. A 12-month period of rebuilding and recovery followed the tsunami, and by late 2005 Phuket was once again thriving.

A turbulent few years for Thailand as a whole has periodically affected tourism around the country. But Phuket, as the most mature tourism market, has survived better than most. Violence in Thailand's southern provinces of Narathiwat, Pattani, Songkhla and Yala failed to reach the island, while

A friendly face behind the bar in Rawai

the political rallies and subsequent army coup in 2006 against ousted prime minister Thaksin Shinawatra were confined to the capital.

Phuket itself witnessed disaster in 2007, when a plane from Bangkok crashed on landing during severe weather, killing 91 passengers.

In recent years, seismic political events in Bangkok have resonated strongly on the small southern island. The anti-Thaksin 'Yellow Shirts' blockaded Bangkok's Government House and Suvarnabhumi Airport in 2008 and the following two years saw pro-Thaksin demonstrators on the capital's streets. A number of them died during the protests. In 2011 severe floods crippled much of Central Thailand and in early 2012 a suspected Iranian bomb plot was foiled in the capital.

Despite these troubled political events, which prompt foreign governments to issue travel warnings concerning Thailand, the popularity of Phuket with visitors has increased. And is it any wonder. It remains a beautiful island, diverse in its attractions. Development continues, with new resorts, private villa complexes and a new marina at Chalong. And there are plans for the expansion of Phuket Airport, with a longer runway to allow for the largest airliners, and a capacity of 12.5 million passengers a year by 2015. Visitor numbers are highly likely to continue upwards into the foreseeable future.

Historical Landmarks

1st century BC Southeast Indian colonists land in Phuket.

16th–18th century European merchants begin to trade in Phuket's tin and establish the island as a haven on India-China trade routes.

1785 Ladies Chan and Mook lead a successful defence against an attempted invasion by the Burmese.

1809–12 The Burmese attack again, driving islanders to nearby Phang Nga for a number of years.

1851–68 Phuket emerges as a leader in the tin-mining industry.

1876 Fights break out during a rebellion of tin miners.

c.1900 A huge fire destroys most of central Phuket Town.

1900–20 Governor Rassada Korsimbi reconstructs Phuket Town, turning it into a modern city.

c.1903 The first rubber tree arrives.

1916 Phuket officially becomes a province.

1970s Phuket moves away from mining and towards tourism.

mid-1980s Phuket's rubber industry takes off again.

1997 The Thai baht is devalued. Thailand enters a three-year recession.

2001 Thaksin Shinawatra is elected prime minister.

2004 A tsunami devastates Phuket, causing many deaths.

2005 Thaksin re-elected in a landslide victory.

2006 The Army stages a bloodless coup. Thaksin is forced into exile.

2007 Thaksin is banned from politics, but a Thaksin proxy, the People Power Party (PPP), wins the election.

2008 Opposition 'Yellow Shirts' occupy Bangkok's Government House and airport. The courts disband the ruling party.

2010 Pro-Thaksin 'Red Shirts' occupy parts of Bangkok. Many people are killed or injured in clashes with the army.

2011 The Thaksin proxy Pheu Thai Party, led by his sister Yingluck, wins a landslide election victory. Yingluck becomes Thailand's first female prime minister.

2012 The government lobbies for constitutional change and an amnesty for the former prime minister, Thaksin.

WHERE TO GO

The island of Phuket is located 850km (530 miles) south of Bangkok, just off the long arm of Thai territory that stretches down the Malay Peninsula. It covers an area of about 540 sq km (210 sq miles). Phuket International Airport is in the north of the island, about 30 minutes by car from the main beaches, which are dotted along the west coast. Hat Patong is the most popular beach resort, the place to head to if you are looking for action. The island's widest choice of accommodation is located here, as well as many restaurants, bars and shops, although nearby Kata and Karon beaches are also gaining in popularity. The capital, Phuket Town, is due east of Patong.

The south and, particularly, northwest coasts of the island are favoured by those looking for a quiet holiday. Some of the most attractive beaches are found here, but most accommodation is resort-style, and there are few other facilities. The east coast has little in the way of beaches, but sailors love it, and there are a couple of luxury marinas.

Transport around the island is mainly by tuk-tuks, which can be found in numbers around the beaches, town centres and main points of interest. Fares are negotiable. Alternatively, car and motorcycle hire is easily arranged through hotels and independent tour companies.

Phuket is surrounded by a number of small, offshore islands that are easily reached by boat from Chalong or Rawai on the south coast. Further afield, Ko Phi Phi, famous as the location of the movie *The Beach*, is only a few hours' boat ride from Rassada Pier in Phuket Town.

A visit to Phang Nga province on the mainland to the north makes an excellent day trip. From there you can kayak

Beware of elephants crossing

Hat Patong

around the limestone pinnacles of Phang Nga Bay, or tour James Bond Island, so-called as it featured in *The Man with the Golden Gun*. The small seaside resort of Khao Lak is a few hours north of Phuket International Airport. It is the easiest access point for the Similan Islands, which offer some of the world's best diving.

Krabi province is around three hours east of Phuket by boat. The main attractions here are Ao Nang beach and an island, Ko Lanta. Both could theoretically be reached in a day, although visits of two days or longer are advisable.

PATONG, KARON AND KATA

Phuket's three main beaches are Hat Patong, Hat Karon and Hat Kata. The most famous of the three, and the hub of the island's activity, is the bold and brash **Hat Patong ❶**. The beach here is crowded with sunburnt bodies under rows of beach umbrellas – even in the low season it is virtually impossible to find a quiet spot on the sand – and the constant barrage of touts from restaurants and tailors trying to entice you into their shops gets annoying.

On the plus side, the location is naturally beautiful: the sea is crystal clear outside the monsoon season, and it's good for swimming or snorkelling (although care should be taken not to get too close to the jet-skis and banana boats whizzing by close to the shore). And there's plenty to spend your money on. The restaurants may be overpriced, but the range of cuisine caters for every palate. And while the nightlife in certain areas is seedy and the prostitution blatant, despite this you can still have a fun and entertaining night. There are transsexual cabaret shows, plenty of bars, running from Thai-style to the ubiquitous Irish-themed pubs, and a couple of decent dance venues.

As Patong was developed early into a commercial centre it doesn't have the beachside resorts found in other locations, and only one hotel, Impiana Resort Patong, is right on the beach.

Slightly north of Patong Beach is the much smaller **Kalim Bay**, which is usually regarded as an extension of Patong, despite officially being a separate area. Although it is fairly rocky and is not recommended for swimming because of its choppy waves, this small strip is picturesque, especially when viewed from above. A few high-class restaurants, including one of Phuket's most famous, Baan Rim Pa *(see page 109)*, are located above the bay.

Soi Bangla (Bangla Road)

Many visitors to Hat Patong make at least one night-time

Seafood and surfing

Hat Patong is the site of the annual Quiksilver surfing contest in September, in which surfers from around Asia compete for prizes. DJs set up on the beach and there are surf clinics and stalls selling delicious food.

Anchoring a boat on Hat Patong

visit to the notorious **Soi Bangla** . The action-packed street and sub-sois (smaller streets leading off it) are a frenzy of bars, pubs, clubs, restaurants and street stalls, with the odd tailor thrown in for good measure. The street is open to traffic throughout the day but becomes pedestrian-only at night, making it a lot easier – and safer – to stumble down. Many of the bars are popular with sex tourists, although the atmosphere is much more relaxed than red-light areas in the west and feels surprisingly safe. While single men may get hassled to buy drinks for the bar girls, women, couples and even families can amble down the street, stop in a bar or two and be treated no differently than they would elsewhere on the island.

The further from the beach you walk, the louder and more intense the activity seems to get. In the centre of Soi Bangla are a number of *katoey* (ladyboy) bars, where members of 'the third sex' dress nightly in elaborate cabaret-type outfits,

complete with feather headpieces and chiselled make-up.
Nightclubs are mostly found at the top of the road, and are
usually located above huge entertainment complexes. **Bangla
Boxing Stadium ❸** (charge; www.banglaboxingstadiumpatong.com), at the far end of Soi Bangla, holds Muay Thai
kickboxing fights featuring Thais and foreigners at 9pm every
Wednesday, Friday and Sunday.

Patong's other attractions

There are gay-friendly hotels, bars and cafés in an area located in
the lanes around the **Paradise Complex ❸** on Rat Uthit Road.

Patong is a great place to shop, and also on Rat Uthit is the
huge shopping centre **Jungceylon** (www.jungceylon.com). It
contains a large number of shops, as well as restaurants, bars,
a cinema and accommodation. Behind is JJ Mall, now with
more shops following renovation after a fire in 2011. It is the
site of a new attraction called **Phuket Slingshot ❹**, in which
people are catapulted into the air in a metal cage attached to
bungee ropes.

Art-lovers should make a trip to **Phrachanukhro Road
❺**, to buy paintings or have them produced to your own
requirements. Stalls also
line the beachside and Soi
Bangla. Similar products
can often be found at a
cheaper price in Phuket
Town, although Patong
usually has a greater selection. Expect to see lots of
custom-made jewellery, fake
designer clothes and handbags, and pirated DVDs.

Simon Cabaret

At the southern end
of Hat Patong is **Simon**

Cabaret ❻ (tel: 0 7634 2011; www.phuket-simoncabaret. com; daily, show times 6pm, 7.45pm and 9.30pm; charge), an entertainment complex offering Las Vegas-style shows featuring Thailand's infamous ladyboys. The shows are popular for their over-the-top routines of lip-synching song and dance routines by performers ranging from cross-dressers to recipients of sex change surgery. You can pay to have your photo taken with the cast afterwards.

Just around Patong's southern headland is **Freedom Beach**, which is much quieter and more peaceful as the only way to reach it is by a 15-minute boat ride. While it has no accommodation, there is seating in front of a row of coconut palms, and a few small restaurants. Rocks and coral close to shore at the southern corner make for some excellent snorkelling.

Hat Karon

A scenic 10-minute drive over a coastal hill to the south of Hat Patong is **Hat Karon**. The 4km (2.5-mile) banana-shaped beach has the advantage of being somewhat less chaotic, while still being close to the action, and with little development near its golden shores it has a much more natural feel.

Domestic nirvana?

Phuket's property market is booming, thanks to an increasing number of expatriate buyers. Dream homes sell at a fraction of what they would cost in Europe, but property laws and ownership regulations for foreign investors change frequently, making a reputable lawyer a must.

A grassy embankment lined with trees separates the beach from the road and hotels. The beach is windswept and often has crashing waves in the rainy season, making it good for surfing. Red flags denoting 'no-swimming' are common across the whole island during the monsoon season (May to late October), but Hat Karon in particular

Hat Karon

seems to be more blustery than most. Snorkelling is excellent around a coral reef at the southern headland, which separates Hat Karon from Hat Kata.

There are shops, and a few bars and restaurants around Hat Karon. Most distinctive is the dining and mini-golf complex **Dino Park ❷** *(see page 96).*

Hat Kata Yai and Hat Kata Noi

Although rapid development has changed the once quiet and intimate image of **Hat Kata**, it is still arguably the most scenic of Phuket's three principal beaches. Hat Kata has the best of both worlds. Although busy, its smaller size and fewer hotels give it a more relaxed feel than Hat Patong, but there is a far greater choice of shops, bars and restaurants than Hat Karon. There are actually two Kata beaches, Hat Kata Yai (*yai* means big), commonly referred to as Kata, and Hat Kata Noi (*noi* means small). Hat Kata Yai is the busier location, where

Sunloungers on Hat Kata

virtually all the accommodation and entertainment are found. The beach itself has fine white sand and clear waters with a hue that changes from deep to light blue throughout the seasons. Some excellent snorkelling can be enjoyed around the headlands to both the north and south.

Hat Kata is quiet and romantic in the evening, with twinkling lights illuminating the strip of beach heading to the north. The famous Boathouse hotel and restaurant are located at Kata and there is a casual reggae-type beach bar to the far south, where chunky wooden tables extend over the sea. The food isn't great here, but they do stage mesmerising fire shows on the sand.

To the south of the headland, **Hat Kata Noi** is much quieter than its neighbour. Under Thai law, no beach can be privately owned, but the Katathani Resort owns all the land directly facing the sands, which means that in practical terms it is usually only the guests of the hotel who use the beach. Hat Kata Noi is similar in appearance to 'big' Kata, with white sand and calm, clear waters.

Kata Hill

Phuket has many viewpoints overlooking the beaches, mountains and Andaman Sea. A number of the more popular ones are located around Hat Kata. Seen on many a postcard is **Three Beaches Viewpoint ❸**, a stunning spot so named for its unique location looking down onto the headlands of Patong, Karon and Kata beaches. Due to the elevated hillside location, clouds tend to build rapidly from lunchtime onwards, so for the best views and photographs of this trio of beaches arrive early in the morning or early in the evening (in time for sunset). The viewpoint is at the peak of Kata Hill, just south of Hat Kata, and is known by all taxi and tuk-tuk drivers.

Kata boasts a number of spectacular places from which to see the sun set into the sea. The After Beach Bar is a wooden reggae bar jutting out over Kata Hill which offers cheap beer, Thai food and a chilled-out atmosphere that is perfect for enjoying the setting sun. A little further along on the opposite side of the road is **Kok Chang Elephant Camp** (www.kokchangsafari.com). Visitors can arrange to go on elephant treks, or just feed the elephants and stop for a drink at the bamboo bar at the front of the park, where they will often be joined by two resident monkeys. For something a little more up-market, visit Ratri Jazztaurant (www.ratrijazztaurant.com), perched high in the hills off Patak Road. Cocktails are the name of the game, as the food is so-so and there's only occasional live jazz. A long walk uphill is required to experience the view, but the golden orb of the sun melting into the horizon over the Andaman Sea is a stunning reward for those who do make the climb.

The view from Three Beaches Viewpoint

Phuket Fantasea

NORTHWEST COAST

As a general rule in Phuket, the further north you go, the quieter it gets, and the undeveloped beaches around the island's northern tip stand in stark contrast to Hat Patong.

Although there are a few mid-range options, accommodation on the northwest coast is generally based around the resorts, which tend to be within the higher price bracket. Outside the resorts, there are far fewer restaurant and shopping facilities than there are around the main beaches, and although those within the resorts themselves are typically of a high quality, the prices reflect this.

But if your budget and tastes run to it, this quieter side of Phuket is well worth experiencing – a place where beaches are less crowded, noise is kept to a minimum, and a busy day involves little other than flipping from your front to your back to ensure an even tan.

Hat Kamala, Hat Surin and Hat Bang Tao

Hat Patong's closest northerly neighbours, which are steadily increasing in popularity, are Hat Kamala and Hat Surin. Those who stay at **Hat Kamala** are blessed with a small yet pristine beach that is peaceful yet well located if they should wish to venture over the hill for a bit of nightlife. Headlands to the north and south shelter the beach, and with forested hills rising inland, the overall effect is a very picturesque bay. Kamala retains something of a village atmosphere.

The stretch of sea-facing land above Kamala is known by locals and foreign investors as 'millionaires' mile'. Expansive villas with picture-perfect views, most worth US$1 million and above, have been carved into the hillsides.

Hat Kamala is the site of **Phuket Fantasea** ❹ *(see page 95)*, a night-time cultural theme park at the foot of the hill dividing Kamala from Surin. A winner of the Thailand Tourism Award for Best Attraction, the complex hosts cirque du soleil-type acrobatic performances and animal shows, one of which features a stage full of elephants.

With its golden rather than white sands, **Hat Surin** looks different from many of Phuket's other beaches. It is nonetheless very scenic, with rows of casuarina trees to the rear. Hat Surin can get pretty busy at peak times, but during the low season it is often deserted. At certain times of year there is a strong undertow, making it more important than ever to pay attention to the red flags that indicate potentially unsafe swimming conditions. Lunchtime offers the opportunity to sample fresh fish and seafood at shaded bamboo tables at one of the many beachfront restaurants.

Another attraction in the area is **Laem Singh**, a tiny bay dominated by rocks between Hat Kamala and Hat Surin. On Sundays many people gather to eat seafood and listen to music being played on the sand.

Kamala and Surin are home to a high concentration of Thai Muslims, and there is therefore a more reserved atmosphere

here. Topless sunbathing, which is disapproved of by Buddhist Thais, is even more frowned upon here. Likewise, there are fewer late-night bars and restaurants here than elsewhere on Phuket. Many of the island's mosques are found inland in the villages around Surin and Kamala.

Heading north, just a few kilometres before the next major beach of Hat Bang Tao is the much smaller **Ao Pansea**. This tiny gem of a bay is rarely visited, as it is mainly accessible only via Phuket's most exclusive resort, the **Amanpuri** *(see page 140)*. The other end of Ao Pansea is anchored by the Surin Phuket resort, which is much more affordable, but still beyond the reach of many. Private residences at the resort are frequented largely by the rich and famous, who are undeterred by the extravagant price tag and lured by the guarantee of seclusion. Movie stars, rock stars and royalty have all vacationed in the private pavilions of the Amanpuri, and security guards do not hesitate to forcefully turn away unwanted visitors.

Phuket's northwest coast is the location for a number of the island's most exclusive hotels and resorts. The renowned **Laguna Phuket** complex consists of five luxury hotels sharing a spa, 18-hole golf course and other leisure facilities, all facing **Hat Bang Tao.** With its Family Fun Zone and Camp Quest activities for children aged 8–12, this is a popular option for family holidays.

Although accommodation runs the length of this 8km-(5-mile) beach, all of it is thankfully low-rise, so Hat Bang Tao retains a relatively secluded feel. There are also several restaurants and antique shops.

The **Phuket International Horse Club** ❺ *(see page 89)* has trekking routes passing through the forests and lagoons around the Laguna Phuket complex, and also has accommodation.

The town of **Choeng Thale**, a few kilometres east of Hat Bang Tao, has shops, bars and restaurants. Prices are a fraction of those charged by the Laguna hotels. Just outside the town, near the Laguna complex, is the original **Hideaway Day Spa** (tel: 0 7627 1549; www.phuket-hideaway.com), which now also has centres in Patong and Chalong. It specialises in Thai massage and pampers clients on open-air Thai *salas* overlooking a peaceful freshwater lake.

Sirinat National Park

A large part of Phuket's northwest cape consists of **Sirinat National Park**, an area of around 90 sq km (35 sq miles) that takes in the beaches of Hat Mai Khao, Hat Nai Yang and Hat Nai Thon. Around three-quarters of the park is marine, extending 5km (3 miles) out to sea, with the rest made up of the adjoining beaches and mangrove forests, in which casuarina trees provide shelter for a diversity of birds, mammals and insects. Sirinat National Park is home to some of Phuket's

Water buffalo and egrets in the Sirinat National Park

most beautiful coral reefs, where plate and tree corals share the waters with sea fans, sea anemones and masses of brightly coloured tropical fish. The **Thachatchai Nature Trail** leading to the park's northern end follows a 600m (1,970ft) long raised wooden walkway. Along the way, signs highlight flora and fauna common to the region.

By far the smallest of the Sirinat National Park beaches is the beautiful but isolated **Hat Nai Thon**. It can be extremely difficult to find, as it is located at the foot of a series of steep hills that require navigation through winding roads, jungle and rubber plantations. Peaceful and quiet, Hat Nai Thon offers sunbathers a tranquil spot in which to relax and has a few sunbeds for hire. Snorkelling conditions are excellent, with rocky headlands sheltered from wind and strong currents attracting marine life year-round. A wrecked tin dredger lies abandoned in the waters at a depth of 16m (52ft), to which

Spas

Many spa treatments that now form an integral part of the Thai travel experience have their roots in Buddhism. When travelling monks came to Thailand in the 2nd or 3rd century AD, they brought *nuad paen boran* (ancient massage), developed, legend says, from Indian Vedic treatments created by the Buddha's own medical advisor. Nearly 2,000 years after it entered the country, the world now calls it simply Thai massage.

The association with religious philosophy means the most dedicated masseurs still perform the service within the Buddhist concept of mindfulness, making a *wai* – a slight bow with hands clasped – to pay respects to their teacher and focus on *metta* (loving kindness), which is thought to be the ideal state of mind in which to give massage.

For centuries, temples were places of healing (many now have hospitals nearby), and they employed several other treatments we now associate with modern spas, such as herbal compresses.

Hat Nai Yang

visits can be organised through the Nai Thon Beach Resort (tel: 0 7620 5379; www.phuket-naithon.com).

Hat Nai Yang ⑥ is the middle of the park's three beaches and is almost deserted in the monsoon season due to its rugged and blustery appearance. The wind and rain, however, take with them the leaves and branches that litter the shores following fierce storms, and by the time high season rolls around, Hat Nai Yang is transformed into a beauty. The lovely curving bay is the location of the headquarters of Sirinat National Park, and, although not nearly as busy as the southwest coast, it is the most popular beach in this area. As there are no hotels directly on the beach itself, Hat Nai Yang maintains an unspoilt feel. During high season, a row of thatched beach huts offering cold refreshments and freshly cooked seafood lines the sand under the shade of evergreen trees. Snorkelling and scuba-diving trips can be arranged to a large coral reef about 1km (half a mile) out to sea, and the

Sea turtle near Hat Mai Khao

occasional nesting turtle will wander ashore from the neighbouring Hat Mai Khao.

Phuket's most northerly beach, **Hat Mai Khao** ❼, is also its longest, at more than 17km (10.5 miles). Yet it is one of the quietest and least developed, although there are several hotels. The most notable names are the JW Marriott Resort and Spa and the sleek and very stylish all-villa Anantara Phuket resort next door. The JW resort, the first to open, was initially criticised for encroaching on national park property, but the resort managed to change public perception by initiating the Marine Turtle Foundation (see below). All guests who stay at the JW resort are encouraged to donate US$1 a day to support local conservation efforts that help ensure the turtles' yearly return to Mai Khao's pristine shores.

Hat Mai Khao remains one of the most beautiful beaches on the island, with huge stretches of almost deserted powder-white sand lapped by some of the clearest turquoise waters.

PHUKET TOWN

Although by no means as popular as the coastal areas, **Phuket Town ❽** offers an eclectic mix of historic buildings, bustling markets and chic restaurants, and is steadily appealing to more visitors as a destination in its own right. Popular sights include stately Sino-Portuguese buildings erected by 19th-century tin-mining tycoons and the mansions of post-war rubber barons. Most of the town works on a one-way grid system that, while difficult to navigate by car, is pretty easy to explore on foot. Given the town's strong Chinese heritage, many businesses close on Sundays.

Colonial architecture

Some of Phuket's finest architecture can be seen in the **Old Town** area around Thalang, Dibuk and Krabi Roads. A

Sea turtle conservation

Hat Mai Khao is home to the Marine Turtle Foundation, which raises funds to help protect the turtles that use Hat Mai Khao as their annual nesting ground. The foundation strives to keep the area free from development to ensure the safe return of the hundreds of Olive Ridley sea turtles and endangered giant Leatherbacks.

Both species come back to the quiet shores where they were born to lay their eggs between November and February each year. If you are here at the right time, you can witness the thousands of hatchlings making their dash across the sand to the sea. The number of eggs laid each year is recorded by local Mai Khao villagers, who patrol the beach during the evenings to guard the nesting sites. A number of eggs are taken to a hatchery to ensure their survival in case of human or natural disturbance of the nests, and the baby turtles are released during a special ceremony in April.

Colonial buildings in central Phuket Town

number of huge colonial-style mansions, Sino-Portuguese shop-houses, and a scattering of other architecturally unique buildings were erected in this area during the 19th-century tin-mining boom, and are well preserved.

Many of the rich Chinese immigrants who amassed their wealth from the mines built mansions for themselves and their families as a display of their prominence and success. These mansions had huge entrances, terraced upper levels and elegant central courtyards. The greater the wealth, the greater the scale of design, and it was not uncommon for some of the most indulgent mansions to have two or even three courtyards.

Commonly regarded as Phuket's most beautiful home, **Phra Pitak Chinpracha Mansion** on Krabi Road has been restored and opened in 2010 as home to a branch of the international Thai restaurant chain **The Blue Elephant Ⓐ** *(see page 113)*. You can get Thai cooking lessons here. The building, named after its original owner Tan Ma Siang, more commonly known as Phra Pitak Chinpracha, was formerly the Governor's Mansion. Next door is **Chinpracha House**, also built by Tan Ma Siang, which is open to the public for tours (tel: 0 7621 1167; Mon–Sat 9am–4.30pm; charge).

The vast majority of Phuket's Sino-Portuguese shop-houses are on **Thalang Road**, where buildings date back to the first half of the 20th century, and on side streets such as Soi Romanee, the old red-light district for tin-mine workers. The traditional and historical values of these buildings spared them from being torn down when Phuket began modernising, and despite being extensively renovated, the original structures still stand. Many shop-houses built during the tin-mining era have been transformed into art galleries, coffee shops and outlets for traditional Chinese herbal medicines. Chinese lettering still appears above many doors, and the pavements are lined with grand arches divided into sections by tall Corinthian-style pillars.

The **Thai Hua Museum B** (tel: 0 7621 1224; www.thaihua-museum.com; daily 9am–5pm; charge) on Krabi Road has wide-ranging exhibits in the garden and in several rooms over two floors, with topics including Phuket traditional ceremonies, Sino-Portuguese buildings and local cuisine. Another restored former residence of Tan Ma Siang, number 20 Thalang Road, is now the popular **China Inn**, a colourful and artistic antiques store, restaurant and garden café decorated in rich Chinese red and gold. Other cultural artefacts are found at the 80-year-old former post office on Montri Road, which

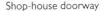

Shop-house doorway

Shop-houses

The Sino-Portuguese shop-houses in Phuket Town are a fascinating taste of old Phuket; they are all alike in design, only 5m (16ft) in width but can stretch back as far as 50m (160ft). The front of each building has a sheltered entrance, and each row is usually divided into five shop-houses.

is now the **Phuket Philatelic Museum** (tel: 0 7621 1020), and at the **Thavorn Hotel Lobby Museum** **C** on Rassada Road (tel: 0 7621 1333; charge), a small family-run hotel museum with historical items ranging from tin-mining paraphernalia to toy trains and opium beds.

Inside the elegant **Phuket Provincial Hall** on Damrong Road is an antiquated courtroom featuring a wooden judge's bench that has been in use for the past century. The Provincial Hall itself, which is just across the lawn, was made famous when it served as the French Embassy in Cambodia in the 1984 film *The Killing Fields*.

Markets and shops

Phuket Town is *the* place to find the cheapest prices at the local markets. For clothes and accessories, the undercover **EXPO Market** **D** on Tilok Uthit 2 Road changes its stock regularly, and usually has something a little different from the markets around the beaches.

Phuket's oldest and largest fresh produce market is on Ranong Road and is bustling throughout the day. The early morning is particularly busy, with locals arriving to select fruit, vegetables, herbs, spices, meat, fish and a host of other ingredients for restaurant and domestic kitchens. Most Thai cookery courses in Phuket will begin with an early-morning visit to this colourful market, which was once frequented by pirates and traders.

One of Phuket's most interesting markets is also its most popular. **Talad Tai Rot**, more commonly known as the weekend market (Sat–Sun, evenings only), is located just outside

Phuket Town. Two roads, Chao Fa East and Chao Fa West, head to the south of the island, and the market is on a road running between them, indicated by a road sign simply stating 'short cut to town'. The market, opposite Wat Nakha, is the local version of Bangkok's Chatuchak and sells everything from clothing and accessories to household items and pets. It has lots of food stalls, too.

Central Festival (daily 11am–10pm) is a large shopping complex on the outskirts of Phuket Town. It is too far from the town or beaches to walk there, so is best reached by taxi (all the drivers know where it is located), a journey of around five minutes from the town centre and 15 minutes from Hat Patong. As well as independent stalls, global franchises, a supermarket and a department store spanning four levels, Central Festival has numerous restaurants, a cinema and a spa.

Figurines in Jui Tui temple

The independently owned boutique within **Siam Indigo Exotique Bar and Restaurant** on Phang Nga Road is more intimate, and features a stunning collection of clothing, jewellery and accessories.

Phuket Town temples

There are temples all over the island of Phuket. The best known is in the Chalong area, aptly named Wat Chalong, but most are in and

Incense bowls, Put Jaw temple

around Phuket Town. Each is unique and often has a history steeped in legend and folklore. Due to a strong Chinese influence resulting from the influx of immigrants during the 19th century, many of Phuket Town's temples are Taoist.

The oldest Chinese temple is **Put Jaw**, on Ranong Road near the town centre. Built over two centuries ago, and dedicated to Kwan Im, the Chinese goddess of mercy, it suffered severe damage in a fire and was renovated around 100 years ago. Although not the island's most architecturally impressive temple, Put Jaw is nevertheless one of the more interesting to visit. An image of Kwan Im stands in the middle hall, surrounded by numerous fortune-telling devices. The simplest of these divining methods involves a pair of red wooden blocks – the idea is to ask a question and let the blocks fall to the floor in front of an altar. A 'yes' or 'no' answer is determined according to which way they land. Alternatively, the 'can and stick' method of divining requires a bit more effort. Two cans filled with numbered sticks are vigorously shaken until one of the sticks falls out. The numbered stick is then taken to a room filled with boxes containing corresponding numbered slips, on which should be written the answer to the question you asked. Paper slips are in Thai, and as few people around the temple grounds speak English you may need to ask elsewhere for an interpretation.

Adjoining Put Jaw is the much more visually spectacular **Jui Tui** Ⓔ temple, dedicated to Kiu Wong In, the Chinese vegetarian god who is worshipped annually during the week-long Vegetarian Festival (see box). Jui Tui is the main temple for the festival. Huge teak doors depicting carvings of guardians lead into the temple, where a dramatic red-faced statue of Kiu Wong In sits on an altar surrounded by offerings of various fruits and vegetables. A red firecracker house was built to the left of the temple in 2011 for people to throw live fireworks in a bid to reduce noise and air pollution.

Erected in 1853, **Sanjao Sam San**, on Krabi Road, is a more peaceful temple, dedicated to Tien San Sung Moo, the goddess of the sea and the patron saint of sailors. Sanjao Sam San has a much more refined ambience, with gold statues of two lions

The Vegetarian Festival

For one week each year during the ninth lunar month, Phuket Town takes on an intensely freakish vibe as Taoist devotees indulge in rituals to prepare their bodies as living sacrifices to the gods. Entering trances, they spear their faces with anything from palm leaves to 2.5m (8ft) steel poles, then pace the streets mutilating themselves with gruesome piercings, slicing their tongues and thrashing their bare backs with axes and machetes. Thousands line the streets to observe the events, which are accompanied by loud music, frenzied dancing and the noise of exploding firecrackers. During the festival, street stalls and markets all over the island sell Thai and Chinese vegetarian food, often fashioned to resemble meat.

on the outside and intricate carvings displayed on the inner walls. Ceremonies are traditionally held in the temple grounds to bless the launch of new boats and to ask for the sailors' safety and protection.

Parks and viewpoints

A public park at **Saphan Hin**, located in Phuket Town where Phuket Road meets the sea, is popular with joggers, who take advantage of the mangrove- and tree-lined trails that wind around it. The park also has a fitness centre, stadium, restaurants and food stalls. A number of festivals and events take place within the park grounds throughout the year and 2011 saw a new attraction: a musical fountain in which the water dances to music composed by the King at 7.30pm, 8.30pm and 9.30pm nightly. Slightly out of the town itself is **King Rama IX Park**, more commonly known as **Suan Luang**. Although not as large as Saphan Hin, Suan Luang is also popular with exercisers. Many people arrive early in the morning to participate in t'ai chi lessons, or to jog around the tree-lined lotus ponds.

You can enjoy panoramas of the southern part of the island from **Khao Rang,** Phuket Town's only real viewpoint. The hill also receives cooling breezes. Tung-Ka Café *(see page 114)*, near the peak of the hill, serves Thai food throughout the day. Bordered by frangipani and bougainvillea, with forest to the sides and above, the area attracts birds during the day and choruses of crickets in the evenings. This can be a

The Buddha statue at Khao Rang

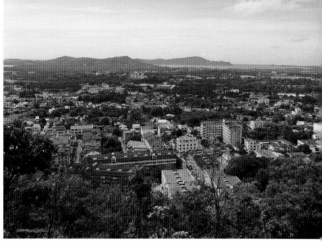

The view from Khao Rang

peaceful place to watch the sun set over the town. A huge 9m (29ft) Buddha statue in the 'suppression of evil' pose is located about halfway up Khao Rang on the northern side.

Northern outskirts

The **Orchid Garden and Thai Village** ❾ (tel: 0 7623 7400; daily 8am–9pm; charge) is a large cultural centre offering Thai dancing and shows, handmade crafts, traditional Thai restaurants and elephant training. This is also the location for glitzy wedding services, with ceremonies steeped in Thai culture and tradition; the bride and groom can even arrive on elephant-back – a Thai version of a horse and carriage.

Butterfly Garden and Insect World (tel: 0 7621 0861; www.phuketbutterfly.com; daily 9am–5.30pm; charge) features more than 40 species of butterfly in a natural rainforest environment and is a peaceful place to spend a few hours. Also on display are large spiders, stick insects and scorpions.

At the Thai Village

A separate enclosure houses rare and native birds of Thailand. Factual displays give details about the species and their natural habitats.

A Phuket version of Bangkok's cultural attraction **Siam Niramit** ❿ (tel: 0 7633 5000; www.siam-niramit.com; Wed–Mon 5.30pm–10pm; charge) opened in Rassada at the end of 2011. As well as facilities such as a floating market, restaurants and tableaux of village life, a spectacular one-hour show starts at 8.30pm highlighting aspects of Thailand's history and culture.

Another Rassada newcomer was the 2012 opening of **The Simon Star Show** (tel: 0 7652 3192; www.simonstarshow.com; charge) in a purpose-built 130-million baht theatre. Its ladyboy lip-synching cabaret shows daily at 6pm, 7.45pm and 9.30pm and includes an underwater sequence.

EAST COAST

Phuket's east coast has not seen the substantial development of the west coast as it has mainly rocky embankments and virtually no beaches. The east coast is popular with sailors, however, and four of Phuket's five marinas are situated there. **Yacht Haven Marina** (www.yacht-haven-phuket.com), in the far north, has few facilities aside from boat moorings, but **Ao Po Grand Marina** (www.aopograndmarina.com), in the northeast, has a bar and restaurants. Both the **Phuket Boat**

Lagoon (www.phuketboatlagoon.com) and **Royal Phuket Marina** (www.royalphuketmarina.com), virtually next to each other on the central east coast, are huge developments boasting exclusive bars and restaurants and luxury waterfront accommodation.

Laem Pan Wa

To the southeast of Phuket Town is the **Laem Pan Wa** peninsula. Accommodation is limited here, although there are some incredibly luxurious developments. It is difficult to reach, so is best suited to those seeking a very quiet and peaceful resort-based holiday. Although remote, Laem Pan Wa is nonetheless very beautiful, with numerous palm-tree plantations and spectacular sea views towards clusters of islands.

Phuket's deep-sea port and naval base are here, as is the **Phuket Aquarium and Marine Biological Research**

Sunset at Laem Pan Wa

Centre ⑪ (tel: 0 7639 1126; daily 8.30am–4.30pm; charge), where there is a walk-through shark tunnel, tropical fish, reefs and a children's touch pool containing starfish and sea cucumbers. Local buses leave for the aquarium from Ranong Road in Phuket Town.

Sailing on the waters around Laem Pan Wa is a wonderful experience, and can be arranged at the **Phuket Yacht Club** at **Ao Yon**, the only real beach on the east coast. Empty stretches of sand leading to curving headlands make it particularly picturesque. Once you get beyond the headlands the winds quickly pick up, which is what attracts so many sailors, but the beach itself is well sheltered and good for swimming year-round.

Khao Khad View Tower ⑫ is often deserted because most people head to the easier-to-reach viewpoints on the opposite

Sea gypsies

The 'sea gypsies', known in Thai as *chao lay*, or 'people of the sea', are divided into three groups, though they sometimes intermarry and generally consider themselves as one kindred people. They live only along the Andaman Sea, either in huts by the shore or on itinerant craft plying coastal waters from Ranong to Ko Tarutao.

Phuket's 500 or so remaining sea gypsies are the island's oldest residents. A few survive by selling shells or beads, but the majority still make a very basic living from fishing. Their diet is largely fish, rice and fruit. Neither Buddhist nor Muslim, they instead worship sea, wind and island spirits, and the spirits of dead sea gypsies are believed to live on 'dead' islands. One legend tells of a sea gypsy woman who turned into a sea turtle, and the animals are revered. Once a year, however, it is permitted to hunt and eat turtle meat, while observing ancient rites. Little is known of the sea gypsies' past as they have no written language or records.

western coast, but it is a fantastic place from which to capture some truly spectacular photographs. A two-level viewing tower sits at the highest point of a steep set of stairs, but the 360-degree views from the top make the climb well worth it. Photomaps highlight the sights below, and there are wonderful views out to sea. Parts of Phuket Town, Ao Chalong and the distant outline of Ko Phi Phi are also visible.

Sea gypsy children

Ko Sirey

The tiny island of **Ko Sirey** ⓭ is separated from Phuket's mainland by a bridge measuring just a few metres. Predominantly home to a community of sea gypsies (*chao lay*), the area is poor in terms of material wealth but rich in cultural appeal. Be sure to ask permission if taking photographs. It was planned to make the island's culture more accessible to visitors with a Sea Gypsy Cultural Centre opening in Baan Laem Tukkae village at the end of 2012.

There is a small beach on the eastern side of Ko Sirey, known as **Hat Teum Suk**. It is not really a swimming beach, however, and is visited mostly by Thai families.

THE ISLAND'S INTERIOR

Phuket's interior is a mixture of developed areas and jungle-filled national parks. The northern town of Thalang is home to some superb temples, while Kathu in the south has some good golf courses.

The half-buried Buddha at Wat Phra Thong

Thalang

Once the administrative centre of Phuket, **Thalang** rapidly lost its prominence with the emergence of Phuket Town, around 12km (7 miles) to its south. Thalang has a somewhat shabby appearance, but it holds much historic significance, and there are a number of attractions.

A large roundabout known as the **Heroines' Monument** ⑭ serves as the gateway to the Thalang district. At the centre of this roundabout are the statues of Lady Chan and Lady Mook, who in 1785 organised the successful defence of Phuket by dressing women as soldiers and making fake weapons to trick the invading Burmese into thinking they were facing a far greater army (*see page 17*). More is revealed about these two women at the **Thalang Museum** (tel: 0 7631 1426; www.nationalmuseums.finearts.go.th; daily 9am–4pm; charge), which houses artefacts, photographs and other information about Phuket's past. A display explains the Burmese invasion in detail, and other exhibits reveal facts about tin mining, the rubber industry and the culture of the sea gypsies.

Around 20km (12.5 miles) north of Phuket Town is **Wat Phra Thong** ⑮ (daily 8am–6pm), situated just off the main airport road, near the Thalang District Office. This famous temple is steeped in legend concerning the half-buried golden Buddha found within it (see box). Only visible from the chest up, this striking statue is said to curse all those who attempt to remove it.

Wat Phra Nang Sang, meaning 'temple built by a princess', was erected on the site of the famous battle in which Lady Chan and Lady Mook defeated the Burmese. Harking back to Phuket's tin-mining era, it holds the world's largest tin Buddhas – three of them. In 1973, tin Buddha heads were discovered hidden inside the stomach of one of them. Also within Wat Phra Nang Sang are a large reclining Buddha, a set of statues honouring Lady Chan and Lady Mook, and the body of a mummified monk. Legend says the temple also has a secret treasure map concealed within the grounds.

Khao Phra Taew National Park

In the northeast of the island, about 4km (2.5 miles) east of Thalang, is **Khao Phra Taew National Park** ⓰, the site of Phuket's largest expanse of virgin rainforest, an area of 22 sq km (8.5 sq miles). The best time to visit is the May to

The legend of the golden Buddha

A young boy and his buffalo are said to have suddenly and inexplicably died many centuries ago, when the animal was tied to a mud-covered spiral jutting up from the ground. When the boy's father went to the site of the catastrophe, he discovered the spiral to be the tip of a Buddha image. Villagers attempted to dig the statue up, but attracted swarms of wasps as a result. Only the head was revealed, and further attempts at digging met with disaster. A shelter was eventually built around it, and for many years peace returned. When the Burmese invaded Phuket in 1785, however, they too attempted to unearth the valuable gold Buddha, but a plague of ants descended on them, biting many to death. Today the original Buddha head is encased in a much larger, golden head and shoulders to protect it from theft or damage, and to protect people from falling under the spiritual powers and dark ancient spell it is thought to embody.

Ton Sai waterfall

late-October monsoon season, when flowers are in full bloom and greenery is more vibrant.

Khao Phra Taew is home to some attractive walks and waterfalls. The most accessible waterfall is **Bang Pae**, a leisurely 20-minute walk from the park's entrance. Most of the walk is flat, but there are a few steep rocks to navigate which can be slippery during the rainy season. The waterfall is popular for a picnic or a refreshing dip, but is neither tall nor particularly free-flowing unless the island has recently experienced a lot of rain. Should you feel up to the walk, **Ton Sai waterfall** lies a further 3km (2 miles) along the same route and is much more striking, although this, too, can cease to flow during the dry season.

The information centre can arrange guided treks around this rainforest, which contains the exceptionally rare Lang Khao species of palm. The tree is fan-like in appearance and stands between 3m and 5m (10–16ft) in height. It is found in only one other place, Khao Sok National Park (on the mainland, a three-hour drive north of Phuket). The guides are useful as without knowing what you are looking for the tree would be easy to miss. Likewise, they will point out tracks and other evidence of nearby animals, which may not be picked up by the inexperienced eye.

The **Gibbon Rehabilitation Centre**  (tel: 0 7626 0491; www.gibbonproject.org; daily 10am–4pm; free) is about a 15–20-minute casual stroll from Bang Pae waterfall. The centre operates on a voluntary basis, relying solely on donations and receiving none of the park fees paid by visitors. Many of the gibbons have been rescued from captivity, as a tourist attraction or pet. They are kept in large enclosures, and although they can be seen from a distance, it is not possible to get too close a view of them as they are being prepared for reintroduction to the wild.

Kathu

As a predominantly residential area, the **Kathu** district has little in the way of accommodation and is not within walking distance of the beaches and entertainment facilities. What is does offer, though, are a number of attractions that are easily accessible from Hat Patong, which is just a 5–10-minute drive away over Patong Hill. At the foot of Patong Hill is **Jungle Bungy** (*see page 89*), where participants can leap from a crane suspended over woodland towards the calm waters of Kathu Lake directly below. On the hill itself are two

Gibbon Rehabilitation Centre

go-kart tracks, one on each side of the road. They stay open well into the evening and are floodlit for night visitors.

Kathu waterfall is best visited between June and October, when water levels are at their highest, the forest is at its greenest and flowers are in full bloom. A trail winds around the waterfall, beginning at an outdoor restaurant that serves refreshments and a basic selection of foods. Near the waterfall is **Phuket Cable Ski** (*see page 89*), where visitors can try water-skiing or wakeboarding on a pulley system that runs around a large lake. Also set around the lakes of Kathu is the Loch Palm Golf Course, one of Phuket's most popular golfing greens (tel: 0 7632 1929). The Blue Canyon Country Club (*see page 89*) is also nearby.

SOUTHERN PHUKET

Southern Phuket offers visitors a quieter getaway than the west coast. There are a number of peaceful beaches, Phuket's most famous temple, Wat Chalong, and some of the best viewpoints and sunset spots on the island.

Conservation projects for visitors

While Thailand is only just waking up to the impact of ecotourism and environmental conservation, more and more people are visiting the country to participate in conservation activities, either exclusively or as part of a beach holiday getaway.

On Phuket, the Gibbon Rehabilitation Project prepares rescued and abused gibbons for reintroduction to the wild, and is in constant need of volunteers (www.gibbonproject.org). In Phang Nga Province, you can volunteer to monitor sea turtle breeding grounds, or help restore local mangroves. Details are at www.losthorizonsasia.com. When volunteering in Thailand, it's important to organise ahead as officially a work permit is required whether or not you are being paid.

Chalong pier

Chalong

Situated 8km (5 miles) from the centre of Phuket Town is **Ao Chalong**. It's a popular location with expats, having a number of bars and restaurants, but the main attractions for visitors are Chalong's temple and pier. The sailing community will benefit from Phuket's newest facility, the Chalong Bay Marina, which was scheduled to launch in 2012.

Ao Chalong is the main base for the island's scuba divers, as is demonstrated by the number of dive operators and water-themed bars and restaurants on the road leading to it. Names to look out for include the Sailors Rest and The Lighthouse. At the extreme southwest of Ao Chalong is **Hat Laem Ka**, a beach that is suitable for swimming but visited primarily by locals.

Wat Chalong ⑱ is the best-known temple on the island and among the largest. It is very popular, and fills with coachloads of visitors. Consequently, it can have a very touristy

Snake farms

Many different species of snake can be seen in the island's snake farms, which have daily shows and milking demonstrations. Shows are at set times throughout the day, but a 100-baht tip can usually secure a private tour with an opportunity to get up close and personal with some of the non-venomous species.

feel, so it is advisable to visit in the early morning or early evening to avoid the crowds. Built in 1837 during the reign of King Rama III, Wat Chalong houses the statues of three monks: Luang Pro Chaem, revered for caring for Phuket's people during the 1876 Miners' Rebellion, and Luang Por Chuang and Luang Por Gluam, highly respected monks who were abbots of the temple during later years. More recently, Wat Chalong has become the first temple in southern Thailand to house the Holy Phra Borom Sareerikatat relic, a piece of Buddha's bones flown over from Sri Lanka.

One of Phuket's most impressive viewpoints is **Ko Nakkerd**, from which the views towards Ao Chalong and the small islands clustered around it reveal a dramatic colour contrast between the turquoise Andaman waters and the dense green island interiors. Fabulous breezes sweep the hilltop. At the peak of the mountain, the 45m-high **Big Buddha ⑲** image was officially completed in 2011, following years of construction.

Asian and African mammals, birds and reptiles are on display at **Phuket Zoo** (www.phuketzoo.com; daily

8.30am–6pm; charge). There are daily elephant, monkey and crocodile shows, and visitors can have their photograph taken with adult tigers.

On the mountain road between Chalong and Hat Kata is **Kinnaree House** (tel: 0 7638 1667; www.phuket-shooting. com; daily 9am–6pm), where shoppers can purchase Thai silks, batik, pearls and silverware. Also within this large complex is a snake farm that features daily cobra shows, as well as several other facilities, including a paintball ground, an ATV (all-terrain vehicle) circuit and the Phuket Shooting Range.

Rawai

Despite being very scenic, with a cluster of offshore islands and calm waters year-round, Phuket's most southerly beach, **Hat Rawai**, is destined never to be as popular as the island's

On a tour with the Phuket Riding Club

other beaches. The shallow waters come right up to the sea wall, so there is no stretch of sand to lie on and the water-covered rocks make swimming impossible. Rawai is famed, though, for its seafood, and a number of vendors line the quay each evening barbecuing fish caught that day. Longtail boats bob in the water, and the atmosphere is one of calmness and tranquillity.

There is a small sea gypsy community to the east of Rawai Beach. Although you may get a few strange looks if you choose to wander around it, if you do so with respect the locals are generally very welcoming. In particular, never take photographs of people without permission.

Treks through the quieter forests and beaches that surround Rawai can be arranged through the **Phuket Riding Club** (*see page 90*). The area's only other inland attraction is the **Phuket Seashell Museum** (tel: 0 7661 3666; www.phuketseashell. com; daily 8am–6pm; charge), which displays 2,000 varieties of shells primarily from Thailand but with a few offerings from across the world. It also sells souvenirs. The shop is open to everyone, but a small entrance fee is payable to get into the museum. Rarities include the world's largest golden pearl, weighing approximately 140 carats, and a 250kg (550lb) shell. There are also fossils on display, with the oldest reputedly dating back 380 million years.

Promthep Cape

Although Kata has a number of fantastic sunset spots, no trip to Phuket is complete without a visit to the most famous, located on the southernmost tip of the island at **Laem Promthep ⑳**. Hundreds and sometimes thousands of people stand at this cape to watch the sun cast its golden light over a tiny offshore island.

Laem Promthep has a small open-air restaurant serving refreshments and Thai food, which is reasonably priced

The spectacular sunset at Promthep Cape

considering it monopolises the area. Views on leaving the cape are breathtaking, with **Hat Nai Harn** to the front – its many boats bobbing around the Royal Phuket Yacht Club – and a collection of white windmills on the hills behind. Hat Nai Harn is reached by following the road around **Nong Han Lagoon**, signposted from the foot of the Kata Hills, or from Rawai. It is a firm favourite with expats who live in the south of the island.

The **Samnak Song Nai Harn Monastery**, which occupies much of the beachfront land, has spared Hat Nai Harn from excessive development. It has fantastic sunsets and because there is only one hotel directly on the 800m (870yd) beach, it is fairly quiet throughout the year. Although there is little to do here in the way of beach activities or motorised water sports, the odd beach bar and restaurant serves refreshments, and a number of small shops sell beach clothing, jewellery and souvenirs.

From December to April the waters are warm and calm, but Hat Nai Harn is often deserted during the monsoon season due to fierce waves and treacherous swimming conditions. Just around the corner from Hat Nai Harn, past the Royal Phuket Yacht Club, is **Ao Sen**, a tiny and picturesque bay that is rarely visited, simply because many visitors are unaware of its existence.

ISLAND-HOPPING

There are dozens of islands in the waters around Phuket. Although some offer tourist accommodation, many are uninhabited, rugged and untouched, with beautiful beaches that are well worth visiting for the day.

The most popular can be reached easily from the south coast of Phuket, on longtail boats hired from Hat Rawai for a

Longtail boats at Hat Rawai

few hours or a full day. Prices vary drastically between seasons, but depending on your ability to barter, a boat will usually cost roughly between 1,200 and 1,500 baht for the day.

Boat drivers double as tour guides, and the best way to see the islands is often to agree a rate and then leave the choice of exactly where to go up to them. If you have any special requirements, such as the need for a restaurant if you have not brought your own lunch, be sure to tell your driver. Travelling time between the islands is no longer than 30 minutes. Keep in mind that sea breezes create a deceptive coolness and the boats are usually without shade, making it advisable to wear plenty of sunblock.

Ko Hae (Coral Island)

Situated 9km (5.5 miles) off the coast of Hat Rawai is **Ko Hae** (Coral Island). Activities such as jet-skiing and banana boats are available from the two adjacent strips of soft sand beach that face mainland Phuket. Waters are clear and calm close to the shore, and become suddenly and dramatically turquoise at about 5m (16ft) out, where the sea floor suddenly dips. Snorkelling is possible just beyond this point above a wide reef.

Vendors line the beachfront selling snacks and refreshments, and sit-down meals can be enjoyed throughout the day at the island's only accommodation, the **Coral Island Resort** *(see page 142)*. The island was actually named after this resort, and not (as most assume) because of the coral in the waters surrounding it. A few seafood restaurants are set back from the beach, but their opening hours vary and sometimes they do not start serving until the afternoon. As there is only one place to sleep, those staying the night will see the island change from a busy beach popular with day-trippers to a serene and secluded location with only a handful of overnight visitors.

Snorkelling off Ko Hae

Ko Bon

The tiny island of **Ko Bon** is a 10–15-minute hop west of Ko Hae. There is no fresh water or electricity here, which has prevented development and helped Ko Bon maintain a natural, rugged appearance. The side of the island facing Phuket offers better sunbathing. The Evason Resort and Spa, which owned this half of Ko Bon for the use of its guests on Phuket, sold both operations in 2012. They were due to re-open under new management in 2013.

The other side of the island, facing away from Phuket, is not as good for sunbathing. It is, however, an excellent spot for snorkellers to inspect starfish, sea cucumbers and crabs in the many rock pools, although they will need to bring their own equipment because there is nowhere to rent masks and fins. There is little on this side other than the open-air Sit Lo Chia Restaurant, which serves Thai dishes and seafood on tables positioned on the rocks, facing towards the open sea. It becomes crowded with tour groups at midday, but if you time your visit for after 2pm you are likely to be one of only a few people around.

Ko Racha

One of the most exclusive of Phuket's nearby islands is **Ko Racha**. Situated 20km (12 miles) south, it can be reached by longtail boat from Hat Rawai or Ao Chalong. There are two parts to the Racha Islands, the uninhabited Ko Racha Noi and the developed Ko Racha Yai.

Ko Racha Yai is home to the five-star resort **The Racha** (*see page 142*), at **Ao Batok** on the northeast coast. Its sea views and vivid blue waters were no doubt the main appeal to developers searching for the perfect offshore site. Guests have complimentary speedboat transfers from Phuket. Numerous day trips to Ao Batok operate during the high season, when the sands can become a bit crowded, but it is nonetheless a stunning location.

Ko Racha Yai is one of Phuket's most popular sites for scuba divers and the waters are generally free of hazard, so are suitable for all levels. Because of this, many dive operators choose it as their prime site. **Bungalow Bay Reef**, offshore from Ao Batok, has sloping reefs brimming with soft corals and tropical fish. Visibility is high and currents are mild, making it particularly good for beginners. Elsewhere on the island are more white-sand beaches and snorkelling spots.

Resting at the bottom of a grassy slope on the eastern coast is **Ao Kon Kare**, a small sandy beach with **Lucy's Reef** within swimming distance, a nickname given to the staghorn coral found here. More experienced divers can explore a wreck submerged in the waters off **Ao Ter** beach at a depth of 23–35m (75–115ft). **Ao Siam**, on the northern coast, is among Ko Racha's quietest spots, and although it is not as good for diving, snorkelling conditions are excellent. Facilities are limited, and shallow waters close to shore deter boats.

Ko Racha Noi has some equally impressive dive sites, but they are mainly suitable only for advanced divers. A shipwreck lies off the island's southwest coast, and stingrays and reef sharks hover around the northern pinnacle. Waters are deep and currents are strong right around the island.

EXCURSIONS FROM PHUKET

Phang Nga Bay

Situated 65km (40 miles) north of Phuket International Airport, **Phang Nga Town**, on the western side of the Malay Peninsula, rests on flat land surrounded by towering rock faces. It maintains a hidden valley feel, away from modern-day development.

Ao Phang Nga

Aside from a scattering of caves and waterfalls, there is little to do on Phang Nga's mainland, with the exception of a visit to **Tham Phung Chang** ㉑ (Elephant Belly Cave). The cave was named for its likeness to the shape of an elephant, with the cave representing the elephant's body and two outcrops forming the tusks. A popular fable tells of a wounded elephant thought to have morphed over time into Tham Phung Chang after dying from a fatal wound. The cave is actually a 1,200m (3,937ft) underground river tunnel, which tour groups navigate daily, using first a rubber dinghy, then a bamboo raft and finally on foot.

With more than 40 islands formed from colossal limestone pillars erupting from the water, the breathtaking **Ao Phang Nga** (Phang Nga Bay) is the main attraction in Phang Nga province. The bay becomes all the more enchanting in the evening, when the moon casts shadows off these towering rocks into midnight-blue waters, creating a dramatic backdrop against the reds, oranges and yellows of the sunset. Phang Nga Bay hides dozens of sea caves, which are best seen by sea canoe. John Gray's Sea Canoe (see page 87) offers a 'Hong by Starlight' trip into the open-air hongs (caves) to watch fireflies appear as the sun sets.

Other popular excursions include **Ko Ping Kan** (Leaning Mountain Island), better known as **James Bond Island** ㉒ because it featured in the 1974 Bond movie The Man with the Golden Gun. Thousands of visitors have posed on the beach with the limestone pinnacle **Ko Tapu** (Nail Island) in the background to recreate the famous shot immortalised by Roger Moore as 007.

All trips and tours around Ao Phang Nga stop at the Muslim fishing village of **Ko Panyi**, where about 500 houses are constructed on stilts over the water, sheltered by a huge rock on one side. **Khao Khien** (Writing Hill) is another common stopping point. Here, colourful sketches of people, crocodiles, dolphins and sharks, thought to be over 3,000 years old, cover the rock walls.

Khao Lak

On the west coast of Phang Nga province is the little beachside resort of **Khao Lak**, which hit the headlines after it was all but destroyed by the December 2004 tsunami. Khao Lak was steadily restored, however, and is once again blessed with a beauty that attracts visitors by the thousands.

Legendary James Bond Island

The approach into Khao Lak is breathtaking, with a winding mountain road giving way to an expanse of palms lining the beachfront, which blend seamlessly into crystal-clear waters. There are, in fact, six beaches, separated only by rocky outcrops. From north to south they are Bang Sak, Pakarang Cape, Khuk Khak, Bang Niang, Nang Thong and Khao Lak.

The official Khao Lak beach is fairly small at just 800m (870yds), and most of the development is around this and the adjacent Bang Niang and Nang Thong beaches. The region is renowned for its water-based activities, with excellent swimming conditions along all beaches, although after the monsoon rains it is advisable to stay near the northern headlands, where underwater currents are less powerful.

The hot and humid **Khao Lak-Laem Ru National Park** (daily dawn–dusk; charge) is slightly south of the beaches.

Hornbills, monkeys and the occasional Asiatic black bear are all residents of the park, and the views from here across granite boulders towards the beaches are fantastic.

Similan Islands

The exquisite **Similan Islands National Park** ㉓ (tel: 0 7645 3272; Nov–May; charge), 60km (37 miles) west of Khao Lak, commonly appears in lists of the world's top 10 dive sites. The waters are home to technicolour corals, tropical fish, turtles, rays and sharks.

The nine granite islands of the Similans are covered in varying degrees of jungle, washed by clear ocean waters and scattered with powdery white sand. Each island has a Thai name and a corresponding number from north to south, in descending order. Ko Ba Ngu (No. 9) is at the northern end of the island chain, followed by Ko Similan (No. 8), Ko Hin Pousar (No. 7), Ko Payu (No. 6), Ko Ha (No. 5), Ko Miang (No. 4), Ko Pahyan (No. 3), Ko Pahyang (No. 2) and Ko Huyong (No. 1).

With the exception of Ko Ba Ngu and Ko Miang, the islands are uninhabited. National park status was awarded in 1982, and any kind of development was prohibited. Fishing was banned in 1987, and mooring boundaries were established to protect the coral reefs and marine life. The only overnight land accommodation is on Ko Miang, where the national park operates 25 air-conditioned bungalows. Offshore, there are many dive sites (*see page 76*).

Snorkeller, Ko Similan

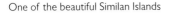

One of the beautiful Similan Islands

Krabi

The province of **Krabi**, to the east of Phuket, spans 4,708 sq km (1,818 sq miles). It is famous for sheer-sided limestone outcrops known as karsts. Their formation began millions of years ago as a result of limestone created by seashell deposits when parts of mainland Krabi were submerged under water. Subsequent continental shifts bulldozed the limestone into the towering peaks. The karsts have appeared in commercials, television programmes and movies, including the 2004 blockbuster *Around the World in 80 Days*. More than 130 islands, many of which are tiny or uninhabited, lie in the waters off the coast of Krabi. The best known are Ko Phi Phi and Ko Lanta.

Of the handful of beaches on mainland Krabi, by far the most popular is **Ao Nang**, which might be pretty if it were not for the longtail boats congesting its beachfront. Ao Nang nevertheless has a laid-back atmosphere, and is the main access point for boat trips to the beautiful Laem Phra Nang peninsula.

Laem Phra Nang (Hat Railay)

Backed by towering limestone cliffs on three sides, **Laem Phra Nang ㉔** (also known as Hat Railay) is one of southern Thailand's most captivating locations. Although a mainland peninsula, it has an island feel as it is accessed only by a 15-minute, 60-baht longtail boat ride from Ao Nang. Its four beaches have crystal waters, powder-white sand and limestone cliffs covered with stalactites dripping into the waters below. This also makes Hat Railay one of the world's leading rock-climbing destinations (look out for the Krabi Rock and Fire International Contest every April).

The main beaches are **Hat Railay East** and **Hat Railay West**. You can walk between them in five minutes along a paved walkway. While Hat Railay West has a perfect strip of fine white sand and clear, warm waters, Hat Railay East is backed by dense mangrove forest and its shoreline is hampered by jagged rocks.

Rayavadee Resort (www.rayavadee.com), among the most expensive accommodation in Thailand and the only occupant of **Hat Tham Phra Nang**, is set amid coconut groves beneath limestone cliffs. There is also access to the beach, though, for daytrippers. At the beach's eastern end the small **Tham Phra Nang** (Princess Cave) has a collection of wooden phalluses offered to the princess's spirit. Look for

Rock climbing at Hat Railay

directions here to **Sa Phra Nang** (Princess Lagoon) and a viewpoint. You'll need good shoes and medium fitness to reach them.

Separated slightly from the rest of the peninsula by a rocky headland, **Hat Ton Sai** emits a greater party vibe than the other beaches, with bungalow-style accommodation and sea-facing bars offering cheap drinks, cheap meals, and starlit fire-eating and flame-throwing performances, against a backdrop of reggae music and painted neon signs. This small bay offers

Similan dive sites

There are over 30 charted dive sites around the Similan Islands. All have good visibility year-round, with clear waters often reaching 18–25m (60–82ft). During high season this can even reach in excess of 40m (130ft).

Christmas Point (Ko Ba Ngu. No. 9). One of the most visually dramatic dive sites in the Similans, with huge underwater boulders, massive sea fans and some of the most extensive coral growth in the area. Fish are plentiful, with small schools of blue travally, jacks and the odd passing shark.

Fantasy Reef (Ko Similan. No. 8). Underwater rock formations dominate this site, a popular resting spot for clownfish and cowtail rays. Depths range from 15 to 40m (50–130ft), usually with fantastic visibility.

Elephant Head (Ko Similan. No. 8). This site attracts some of the ocean's most striking inhabitants, from yellow goat fish, snappers, coral trout and lion fish to reef sharks and the occasional turtle. There are dazzling swim-throughs the deeper you go, and intriguing topography with numerous penetrable holes.

East of Eden (Ko Payu. No. 6). This is an inspiring site with a concentration of marine life unparalleled elsewhere on the east coast. Among the rarer species are pink frogfish.

A longtail boat at Phi Phi Don

amazing views of the open sea, broken in the foreground by a cluster of rocky karsts.

Many of the 650 or so rock-climbing routes across Krabi's cliffs are around Hat Railay. Views are awe-inspiring, taking in mainland Krabi and extending far out to sea. Experienced climbing guides are available across Railay, but are predominantly located at Hat Ton Sai. Krabi waters are now more accessible to sailors after the first phase of **Krabi Boat Lagoon Marina** (tel: 0 7565 6017; www.krabiboatlagoon.com) opened in 2012.

Ko Phi Phi

The twin islands of Ko Phi Phi Don and Ko Phi Phi Ley, collectively known as **Ko Phi Phi**, are roughly equidistant from both Phuket and mainland Krabi. They are the largest islands in an archipelago; the remaining four, Ko Bida Nok, Ko Bida Nai, Ko Yung (Mosquito Island) and Ko Mai Phai (Bamboo Island), are simple limestone formations.

Rayavadee resort, Hat Railay

Ko Phi Phi Don

Ko Phi Phi Don resembles two islands joined by a narrow isthmus, where lies the main pier at **Ton Sai Village,** which is crowded with shops, bars and eateries. A 20-baht charge is now levied to stay on the island. The chilled daytime atmosphere in Ton Sai becomes wild and energetic with the setting sun, when people flock to evening fire shows, beach bars and clubs, including the island's largest nightspot, **The Reggae Bar** – an open-air complex with five long bars, an open-roof dance floor, and a Thai boxing ring where kickboxing fights are staged nightly.

At the other end of the isthmus is **Ao Lo Dalum**, just a five-minute walk away (there are no roads and no transport on Phi Phi). It's blessed with a stunning natural setting wrapped by palm-covered rock formations. A scattering of limestone rocks project from the water and waves roll to shore with a gentle lap.

Most accommodation is clustered around these two beach-fringed bays. For spectacular panoramic sea views, climb up to the viewpoint between them at a height of 186m (610ft).

Around the corner from Ao Lo Dalum and inaccessible by land is **Monkey Bay**. The troops of monkeys that occupy the shores are used to human visitors, and arriving with a few bananas can secure a friend for life – or at least for as long as it takes to get a good photo.

The quietest and most exclusive of Phi Phi's beaches, **Hat Laem Tong**, is at the northernmost tip of the island. It faces **Ko Mai Phai** (Bamboo Island) and **Ko Yung** (Mosquito Island), both of which offer excellent snorkelling and wind-surfing conditions, with flat, calm waters and consistent winds. A small community of sea gypsies also lives here. There is a morning ferry between here and Ton Sai. Otherwise, all transport is by hired longtail boat.

Hat Yao (Long Beach) has powder-white sands and capti-vating views towards Ko Phi Phi Ley, plus a decent range of accommodation. The snorkelling here, above coral, is some of the best on the island. At **Hin Bida** (Shark Point), around 200m (650ft) from the shore, schools of black reef-tip sharks gather in the greatest number in the mornings and evenings.

Ko Phi Phi Ley

Covering just 6.5 sq km (2.5 sq miles) in area, the uninhabited **Ko Phi Phi Ley** is 4km (2 miles) from the larger Ko Phi Phi Don and is encircled almost entirely by steep pinnacles, which provided much of the backdrop for the film *The Beach*. The breathtaking **Ao Maya** ㉕ (Maya Bay) was the film's main location. Sheltered on three sides by rock faces 100m (330ft) tall, it hides several small beaches, some of which are so tiny they are only revealed at low tide. Opposite Ao Maya on the western coast is **Ao Pileh**, which like Ao Maya is characterised by dra-matic vertical cliffs.

The **Viking Cave** ㉖ is fabled as the one-time stop-ping-off point for smugglers and pirates seeking shelter

Lanta's lantern

At the southernmost tip of Mu Ko Lanta Marine National Park is a viewpoint on which rests a small white lighthouse. Framed by both sea and mountain, and facing Ko Rok and Ko Phi Phi Ley, this lighthouse has come to stand as Ko Lanta's island symbol and makes for an ex-cellent photo opportunity.

from the monsoon season. Although some dispute the claim, ancient paintings on the rock walls of Arabian and European sailboats, Viking ships and Chinese junks do seem to imply past visitors of some sort. The most notable attraction today is the sight of swallows' nests, which are harvested annually by locals, who scale the walls on spindly bamboo ladders. The nests are exported to China as the main ingredient in the controversial delicacy bird's nest soup.

Ko Lanta

Ko Lanta Yai (referred to as Ko Lanta) is the largest of an archipelago of more than 50 islands. It is 27km (17 miles) in length and 12km (7 miles) in width. The sea gypsies, among the first settlers on the island, initially named it Pulao Satak, which translates as 'island with the long beach'. True to its name, the nine beaches that span the west coast do give the appearance of one giant stretch of sand. All of them witness glorious sunsets, and contain virtually all the island's facilities. The eastern side of the island is much more rugged, and worth exploring if you fancy getting off the beaten track.

The view towards Ao Lo Dalum and Ao Ton Sai

A hilly backdrop and lines of coconut palms make the far northwestern beaches of **Hat Khlong Dao** and **Ao Pra Ae** particularly picturesque. One of the island's best snorkelling spots is **Hat Khlong Khong**, where low tide exposes small fish that gather around the rocky seabed. Hat Khlong Khong has a distinctive backpacker vibe, with basic bungalows, beach bars and evening fire shows.

Ao Maya, the main location for the film *The Beach*

The adjacent central beaches of **Hat Khlong Nin** and the smaller, more secluded **Hat Khlong Hin** are accessed via a slight detour from the main road. At the start of Hat Khlong Nin is the Rasta Baby Bar, an atmospheric reggae bar displaying the obligatory red, green and yellow Rasta flags and filled with scattered floor cushions. This is the first of a number of similar bamboo bars, which span the length of the beach.

The Pimalai Resort and Spa, Ko Lanta's first five-star resort, dominates the 900m (980yd) stretch of sand at **Ao Kantiang**. This quiet bay is marked by golden sand, calm waters and steep cliffs jutting out to the sides. There are only a few other small developments on Ao Kantiang, with the Same Same but Different restaurant at the southern end attracting the most visitors.

A cluster of undeveloped bays sits at the end of dusty dirt tracks to the island's south. **Ao Khlong Chak**, measuring just

Lighthouse at Mu Ko Lanta Marine National Park

400m (440yds), embodies tranquillity, with very little accommodation, or noise. The even more remote **Ao Mai Phai** (Bamboo Bay) is yet more isolated, and combines deep waters ideal for swimming with shallow rock pools at the northerly edge, which are more suited to snorkelling.

This is the last beach before the start of **Mu Ko Lanta Marine National Park**, which covers the southern tip of Ko Lanta and an additional 15 small surrounding islands. Two mainland beaches fall within the national park, **Laem Tanode** and the rugged **Hat Hin Ngam**, where the park headquarters are situated. A 2.5km (1.5-mile) cliff trail originates from here – keep an eye out for fruit bats, wild deer and reptiles, including monitor lizards and snakes.

Snorkelling and scuba diving
Ko Lanta is the access point for one of Thailand's best snorkelling sites – the brightly coloured square-kilometre coral

reef of **Ko Rok** ㉗. Nearby are the twin peaks of **Hin Daeng** (Red Rock) and **Hin Muang** (Purple Rock), where whale shark sightings are among the highest in the world. These two pinnacles are smothered with red, pink and purple corals, and water temperatures are perfect for the 100-plus types of tropical reef fish that have been catalogued here. Other dive sites accessible from Ko Lanta include Hin Bida, Ko Waen and the *King Cruiser* wreck, a car ferry that sank without fatalities in 1997.

Inland attractions

An elevated hillside spot known simply as **The Viewpoint** is a magical place to see the sun rise. Head to the blissfully silent Khao Yai Restaurant, surrounded by nothing but trees. As the sun peeks above the horizon, it gradually transforms the sky from pitch-black to soft blues, revealing, one by one, the gravestone-like profiles of limestone cliffs, until the sea is filled with them. Hawks and eagles float freely alongside the restaurant's bamboo platform, seemingly staring out to sea along with you.

To the southeast of the island, a winding road leads past rice paddies, prawn farms and fields of wild buffalo to **Lanta Old Town**. This is home to Chinese merchants, Thai fishing families, and a small community of Ko Lanta's remaining indigenous people at a 500-year-old sea gypsy village. Modest shop-houses and shacks on stilts at the water's edge make a stark contrast with the luxurious resorts of the west coast.

Thai girl in Ko Lanta

WHAT TO DO

Phuket boasts a wide range of indoor and outdoor activities to suit all ages. Be sure to check in advance for details of festivals at your time of travel. Many are extravagant, unique and well worth witnessing.

SPORTS AND OUTDOOR PURSUITS

The island's main attractions are its sandy beaches and sapphire water, and many visitors are content to take part in no physical activity beyond the flipping of book pages and basking in the sun. But Phuket has more to offer than relaxation and a guaranteed tan.

You can hire boats, jet-skis and surfboards along many of the main beaches, or ride on banana boats and rubber rings. Hat Patong is the best place for jet-skis and parasailing. Surfboards and windsurfers can also be hired there and at Hat Kata. If renting a jet-ski, look for operators who are insured (there should be a sticker on the side of the craft) and use a life vest. Remember that, strictly speaking, you are not allowed to ride a jet-ski without a licence, and that jet-skis move quickly – accidents do happen.

Ko Phi Phi, Ko Lanta and Krabi and a number of smaller islands to the south can be visited by longtail boat or speedboat on day trips or longer, which might be combined with diving, snorkelling, big-game fishing or water-skiing. Alternatively tour the hidden lagoons of Phang Nga by sea canoe or the mainland jungle terrain by elephant, foot and canoe.

For gentler pursuits on land people head to some of the finest golf courses in Thailand. But for a rush of adrenalin try

Scuba gear on a dive boat in the Similans

Canoeing at Phang Nga Bay

Jungle Bungy at the base of Patong Hill or one of the area's two go-kart tracks. There are also ATV circuits, paintball and a shooting gallery on the island. And if that's not enough, how about climbing through the ropes of a Thai boxing ring?

Water sports

Game fishing. One of the longest-established operators, Wahoo (tel: 0 7628 1510; www.wahoo.ws), offers some of the best day trips and charters. Phuket Deep Sea Fishing (tel: 08 7269 7383; www.phuketfishingcharters.com) has day and night fishing trips on a good choice of boats. It has a strict catch-and-release policy for big-game fish.

Island hopping. Hopping between Phuket's many offshore islands is great fun. The ones nearby can be accessed on longtail boats bargained for at the quayside, but for outlying islands, more speed and, frankly, a bit more swank, speedboats are the best option. Coral Seekers (tel: 0 7622 1442; www.

coralseekers.com) has a wide choice, including Phi Phi, Krabi and Phang Nga. Operators should help you customise a tour depending on how many islands you want to visit.

Sailing. Private and group charters, as well as guided day trips, can be arranged through Sunsail Phuket (tel: 0 7633 6212). Topper Sail Phuket (tel: 08 5215 9185; www.toppersailphuket. com) has a range of dinghies either for fun sailing or lessons for all levels up to regatta training. It also rents out and sells dinghies. The Phuket Raceweek regatta (www.phuketrace-week.com) at Rawai each July and the King's Cup Regatta (www.kingscup.com) at Nai Harn Beach every December attract international sailors and offer chances to crew. For something a little different try sunset sailing in Phang Nga Bay on the Chinese junk *June Bahtra* (www.asian-oasis.com).

Sea canoeing. Sea canoeing is extremely popular around the hidden coves of Phang Nga Bay. The low-lying craft enable you to slip through sea tunnels under the limestone karsts to hidden lagoons and caves, or hong, within. The karsts support their own mini ecosystems, including troupes of monkeys that reportedly swim from island to island. Trips are suitable for most ages, with no experience necessary. They include guides, food and refreshments. Most operators have several programmes. John Gray's Sea Canoe (tel: 0 7625 4505-6; www.johngray-seacanoe. com) offers a starlight trip during which you can launch *krathongs* (candles on banana-leaf floats) into the water, while Sea Canoe (tel: 0 7652 8839; www.seacanoe.net) has overnight excursions with camping.

Scuba diving. There are dive centres all over the island.

Wreck diving

The *King Cruiser*, a 3,000-tonne car ferry, veered off course on 4 May 1997, hitting the Anemone Reef, 32km (20 miles) off the coast of Phuket, and sinking to the ocean floor within an hour. No lives were lost. Scuba divers can visit the wreck from Ko Lanta.

The majority have multilingual instructors who offer first-time explorer dives, as well as PADI (Professional Association of Diving Instructors) certification. Courses involve classroom theory and practical training in both a swimming pool and open water. Dive Asia (tel: 0 7633 0598; www.diveasia.com) on Kata Beach and Scuba Cat Diving (tel: 0 7629 3121; www.scubacat.com) at Patong have a full range of courses and trips, both day-long and live aboard, to most surrounding dive spots, including Ko Racha, Phi Phi, Shark Point and the Similans.

Snorkelling. Phuket's only notable snorkelling spots are at Kata Yai and Kata Noi beaches, where shacks along the sand rent snorkelling gear by the day or hour. Many hotels rent snorkel equipment, as do the numerous dive shops and rental booths along other beaches. Better snorkelling can be found on trips to nearby islands and most dive operators offer a cheaper snorkelling-only option.

Safety by the sea

Phuket's waters are generally very calm, and it is usually only outside the high season that they become choppy (high season is November to April). Lifeguards patrol the main beaches, and the internationally recognised coloured-flag system is always in use – a red flag means do not swim, regardless of how the sea looks. Particularly during monsoon season, surface waters that appear calm can mask strong underwater currents; around a dozen tourists drown each year. Do not risk becoming a statistic – if you see a red flag, do not go in the water. Should you become caught in a rip, do not try to fight it. Swim parallel to the beach until you are out of the rip and can make your way back to shore safely.

Sea breezes and high humidity mask the sun's full power, making heatstroke, sunstroke and severe sunburn common. Use a higher-factor sunblock than you think you need, and avoid the midday sun. It's best to acclimatise slowly and spend plenty of time in the shade when you first arrive.

Water-skiing and wake-boarding. Situated in central Kathu, Phuket Cable Ski (tel: 0 7620 2525; www.phuketcableski.com) is built around a freshwater lake and uses a pulley system to guide its cable skiers. Speedboat operators such as Coral Seekers have facilities for water-skiing, including kneel boards, wake boards and trainer boards.

Land-based activities

Bungee jumping. At Jungle Bungy Jump near Patong (tel: 0 7632 1351; www.phuket-bungy.com) daredevils leap from a crane towards the waters of Kathu Lake below.

Horseriding is popular

Go-karting. Also near Patong, Go Kart Speedway (tel: 0 7632 1949; www.gokartthailand.com) has go-karts and off-road buggies. It stays open well into the evening and is floodlit for night visitors.

Golf. Phuket has several excellent courses, with Blue Canyon Country Club (tel: 0 7632 8088; www.bluecanyonclub.com) among the best. It has two award-winning 18-hole championship golf courses, as well as an on-site spa. Another top course with its own spa, plus beautiful views, is Red Mountain (tel:0 7632 2000; www.redmountainphuket.com). Golf clubs can be hired from some courses, most places offer tuition and green fees include caddy service.

Horseriding. There is horseriding at The Phuket International Horse Club (tel: 0 7632 4199; www.phukethorseclub.com) at

A young Thai boxer in Phuket

Hat Bang Tao and the Phuket Riding Club (tel: 0 7628 8213; www.phuketriding-club.com) in Rawai, which also has a dressage ring. Both cater to all levels and have a choice of forest and beach-front trekking routes. Early morning and late afternoon are generally best to avoid the hottest part of the day.

Jungle safaris. You can get a taste of the ancient rainforest environment on treks such as those run by Elephant Hills (tel: 0 7638 1703; www. elephant-hills.com), who will arrange transfer from Phuket to their tented camp in Khao Sok National Park. From there you have several multi-day options that include day and night safaris, elephant trekking and river canoeing through the mangroves.

Muay Thai (Thai kickboxing). Camps across Phuket such as Tiger Muay Thai (tel: 0 7636 7071; www.tigermuaythai.com) offer various training programmes and spectators can see fights at several stadiums, including Bangla Boxing Stadium, Hat Patong.

Shooting. As well as guns, Phuket Shooting Range (tel: 0 7638 1667) has paintball, archery and karting.

Spas

All across the island small street-side shops offer Thai massage and foot reflexology, while luxurious spas have a wide menu of wellness and beauty treatments. The centres will provide a loose shirt and trousers for Thai massage, which lasts one or two hours. Foot reflexologists apply pressure to specific points on the sole of the foot, which are believed to correspond to internal organs or body parts. Popular spas include Hideaway Day Spa (*see page 39*), JW Marriott's Mandara Spa (tel: 0 7633 8000; www.mandaraspa.com) and Atsumi Healing Centre (tel: 08 1272 0571; www.atsumihealing.com), which includes detox programmes among its treatments.

SHOPPING

Antiques. Rare pieces can be found in shops across the island, with prices ranging from a few hundred to a few million baht. Most shops specialise in Thai artefacts, but some stock rarities from all over Asia. Look out for Ming-style vases from China, Vietnamese lacquerware, and silver from China and Pakistan. Be aware that fakes are common and antiques require an export permit to be taken out of the country. The export of any images of Buddha is prohibited.

Art. Talented artists copy famous masterpieces and will produce paintings based on your photos at a number of galleries on Phrachanukhro Road in Hat Patong. Original works are more expensive, but emerging artists frequently hold exhibitions. Check local newspapers for details. Crafts items are also common. Try Siam Ceramic Handmade (tel: 08 1537 6071; www.thaibenjarong.com) in Patong for traditional ceramics.

CDs and DVDs. Stalls sell pirated music and movies all over the island. Quality varies, although discs can usually be tested before they are purchased. Bear in mind, though, that pirated CDs and DVDs are illegal.

Copied designer items. Clothing, handbags and watches are among the most frequently copied items in the tourist markets. Some are obviously fake; others are surprisingly well

Thai massage

Thai massage differs from traditional Western massage. Its practitioners concentrate more on the manipulation of pressure points and stretching of limbs than on relaxation and kneading muscles.

reproduced. Bear in mind that these fakes are illegal, but if you do decide to buy, always haggle from the original asking price.

Department Stores. The vast Central Festival (tel: 0 7629 1111; www.centralfestivalphuket.com), on the outskirts of Phuket Town, has restaurants, cinemas and a bowling alley as well as shops selling chic fashion, beauty, home decor, electronics, and anything else you can imagine. Jungceylon (tel: 0 7660 0111; www.jungceylon.com) in Patong and Ocean Shopping Mall (tel: 0 7622 3057; www.phuketoceangroup.com) in Phuket Town and Patong also have a wide choice in one location.

Fashion. Department stores sell clothing and accessories, but nowhere is cheaper than the local clothing markets. EXPO Market, in Phuket Town, on Tilok Uthit 2 Road, is one of the better ones, and bargains can always be found at the weekend night market, where jewellery often sells for as little as 20 baht. The French-owned boutique within Siam Indigo Exotique Bar and Restaurant on Phang Nga Road, Phuket Town, is well worth checking out for unique items of clothing, jewellery and accessories.

Food. There are fresh and dried spices and smooth mounds of *kapi* (crushed shrimp paste) and curry pastes prepared before your eyes at the fresh food market on Ranong Road in Phuket Town. Arrive early for the best tropical fruits and vegetables.

Gems. Gem stores stock jade from Myanmar (Burma), gold from India and Sri Lanka, and sapphires and rubies from mines within Thailand. Be prepared to haggle.

Tailor-made clothes. Phuket is full of tailors offering quick and inexpensive made-to-measure outfits. Always bargain and expect a big reduction for larger orders. Thai silk is extremely popular, but there are also rolls of cotton, wool and linen stacked from floor to ceiling. Tailors all have clothing catalogues, and are happy to copy clothes from pictures or items you already have.

Thai silk and fabrics. Ban Boran Textiles in Phuket Town stocks fabrics from six Asian countries. Most famous for Thai silk, however, is the Jim Thompson empire, which has an outlet in Central Festival (tel: 0 7624 9616; www.jimthompson. com) and several others around the island. Materials are usually bought by the metre, although some items may be off the rack.

ENTERTAINMENT AND NIGHTLIFE

A show at Simon Cabaret in Patong

Phuket nightlife in key tourist areas has the high profile energy you might expect from a holiday destination, although bars at some of the quieter beaches close early. Patong in particular always has more than its fair share of all-night offerings. There's a small scene in Phuket Town, Karon and Kata beaches, but more subdued. Elsewhere on the island, nightlife is almost non-existent.

Bars and clubs

For the real action, Hat Patong has the largest, loudest and greatest range of nightlife, with the focus mainly on cheap drinks, happy hours and booming music. But elsewhere on Phuket there are quiet, classy wine bars and casual sunset bars facing the beaches. Although the law states that entertainment venues must close by 1–2am, depending on their licence, the reality is determined by the current climate of local politics and policing. Many clubs in Patong, especially, do not get busy until the early hours. The choice in Patong is wide, with heaving clubs and sex shows on one street, trendy cocktail bars on the next. Most of the scene is along Soi Bangla and its tiny side streets. Most common are raucous open-air 'beer bars', with wooden tables, stools, and skimpily dressed bargirls. One of the best clubs,

Fresh produce for sale at a Phuket Town street market

Seduction Disco (www.seductiondisco.com) has a chunky sound system and regular imported acts. Good bars include Joe's Downstairs (tel: 0 7661 8245; www.baanrimpa. com), a small, classy bar and restaurant decorated in white, with open-air tables jutting over the rocky seafront just north of Hat Patong, and Irish themed pubs like Molly Malone's (tel: 0 7629 2771; www.mollymalonesphuket. com) for pub food, TV sport and live music.

The nightlife in Phuket Town has a more local than tourist atmosphere and is getting livelier, with people heading to bars around Yaowarat Road like the

young and hip Sanaeha
(tel: 0 7621 8514), with its
live music and glitzy chan-
deliers, and the absolutely
packed Timber Hut (tel: 0
7621 1839), a pub with live
Thai rock bands.

On other beaches, Hat
Karon has Angus & Arfur
O'Tool's (tel: 0 7639 8262;
www.otools-phuket.com)
for cold draught Guinness and an excellent Irish-style breakfast, and the family-friendly Harry's Restaurant & Pub (tel:
0 7639 8258), with kid's activities, quiz nights and weekend
all-you-can-eat buffets. Sophisticates at Hat Kata will sip cocktails or one of 24 wines by the glass to the setting sun at The
Boathouse (tel: 0 7633 0015; www.boathousephuket.com),
then possibly rough it down on the beach for late-night reggae sounds and fire shows at Ska Bar (tel: 0 7893 4831).

Cinema

Cinemas can be found inside the Central Festival and
Jungceylon shopping centres. As well as standard seats, there
are reclining sofa seats and a separate 'first-class cinema', where
the ticket price includes drinks and snacks in a welcome
lounge, and a huge reclining comfy chair.

CHILDREN'S PHUKET

Tour companies can advise on trips especially suited to children, and many of the larger hotels have excellent on-site kids'
clubs that can normally be used by non-guests for a small fee.

The award-winning **Phuket Fantasea** (tel: 0 7638 5333;
www.phuket-fantasea.com; daily Fri–Wed 5.30–11.30pm,

Phuket Aquarium

show time 9pm; charge) is a 57-hectare (140-acre) complex at Kamala that advertises itself as a night-time cultural theme park. There are opportunities for photographs of loved ones riding elephants or holding tiger cubs. The nightly show combines acrobatics, pyrotechnics, illusions and performing animals.

Dino Park (tel: 0 7633 0625; www.dinopark.com; daily 10am–10pm; charge), on the hill between Kata and Karon beaches, is prehistorically themed, with stone tables, draping vines, and staff dressed in Flintstones costumes. Golfers on the mini-golf course pass bellowing dinosaurs breathing smoke from their nostrils.

Siam Safari (tel: 0 7628 0107; www.siamsafari.com) and **Island Safari** (tel: 0 7625 5021; www.islandsafaritour.com) offer enjoyable and educational sightseeing tours, incorporating elephant- and ox-riding, monkey shows and demonstrations of rubber-tapping and coconut-milking.

The **Phuket Aquarium and Marine Biological Research Centre** (daily 8.30am–4pm; charge; tel: 0 7639 1128) is home to a number of marine species found in the waters surrounding Phuket. Sharks, rays and tropical fish can all be seen without getting wet and there is a touch pool featuring starfish and sea cucumbers.

Calendar of Events

Some festivals are lunar so dates may vary slightly each year.

February Full Moon: Maka Puja. Candlelit temple ceremonies nation-wide mark the spontaneous gathering of monks to hear the Buddha preach.

13–15 March: The Phuket Heroines' Festival. This fair, with performances, commemorates the two women who organised the defence of Phuket against the Burmese in 1785.

April: Phuket Pride. Week-long gay pride events around the island culminate in a parade at Patong.

April: Phuket Bike Week, Patong. Motorbikes, bands and tattoo shows.

13 April: Turtle release festival. The release of baby turtles into the sea at Mai Khao and Nai Yang Beaches.

13–15 April: Songkran (Thai New Year). Nationwide festival with a party atmosphere and big water fights, based on traditional water-sprinkling rituals for merit-making in temples.

13–15 May: Loy Reua. Sea gypsy festival to mark the beginning of the monsoon season. Offerings for the gods are placed inside model boats and cast away to remove bad luck.

May Full Moon: Visakha Puja. The holiest of Buddhist ceremonies, commemorating the birth, enlightenment and death of the Buddha.

July Full Moon: Asanha Puja. Celebration of the Buddha's first sermon.

September: Quiksilver surfing competition at Patong.

Mid- to late October: Vegetarian Festival. *(See page 49).*

November: Laguna Phuket Triathlon. International competitors line up for swimming, biking and running races.

1 November: Patong Carnival. Festival to mark the beginning of high season, with parades and contests.

November Full Moon: Loy Krathong. Floral baskets filled with candles are floated across seas, rivers and lakes to pay respects to water spirits and welcome the end of the rainy season.

1st week December: Phuket King's Cup Regatta. Week-long regatta at Nai Harn Beach, featuring yachts from around the world.

5 December: King's Birthday.

EATING OUT

Thai cuisine is known globally for its fragrant aromas, delicately blended spices and fiery chilli kick. But those with a more delicate palate should not worry as there are many mildly spiced Thai dishes. Should you overdose on chillies, take a tip from the locals and cool your mouth with plain steamed rice; it's much more effective than water. Most Thai dishes are quick and simple to make, and often contain just a few key ingredients, which when correctly combined create the illusion of a lot more.

THAI FOOD

The careful selection and delicate preparation of fresh ingredients is central to Thai cuisine, and an early morning stroll through the fresh food markets of Phuket will show just how important an act the selection of ingredients is. A visit to the markets is typically the first part of a Thai cookery course. The abundance of market produce and the colourful displays are a delight to see; you can choose from fresh herbs, spices and mounds of pastes for soups, curries and stir-fries, which these days are often market-bought rather than home-made.

The heavier, richer and often spicier cooking style native to the Muslim-dominated southern provinces

Sunday buffets

Sunday buffets are a feature of Phuket, with many hotels offering an all-you-can-eat option. Two that stand out are the Twin Palms buffet, famous for its chocolate fountain, and Hilton Phuket Arcadia Resort & Spa, which has a kids' club, so you can enjoy the feast in peace. Make a booking a few days in advance to ensure a table.

A delicious Thai red curry

has found its way to Phuket, although dishes of the deep south, such as the very hot, deep-orange, chilli- and turmeric-based *gaeng choo chee pla* (sour fish curry), are usually found only in remote local restaurants, or at shopping centre food courts.

Southern Thai curries are pungent and aromatic, often relying on dried and roasted spices. Best-known is *massaman*, a thick, sweet curry prepared in a peanut base and combined with meat (most commonly chicken), potatoes and often either peanuts or cashew nuts. While other curries are served with rice, *massaman* is sometimes served with roti, a fried pastry-like bread. Other traditional Thai curries are a lot lighter, often prepared in a base of fresh coconut milk, delicate herbs and roots, and flavoured with certain blends of spices.

Another exception to this rule is *penang*, a curry similar to *massaman* for its peanut base and creamy consistency, but which is more spicy than sweet and usually only contains

A sea gypsy meal near Hat Rawai

meat, with no added vegetables or nuts. Most restaurants will adapt their dishes, toning down the level of heat if you require it (ask for '*mai phet, khap/kha*', not spicy, please). Many menus in tourist areas will mark the level of spiciness on the menu, and unless you order an obviously spicy dish or specifically ask for chilli, the level of heat is not usually overpowering.

Aside from traditional Thai food, Phuket has innumerable international restaurants featuring cuisine from across the globe. From budget to expensive, it is hard not to find something to suit any culinary desire. Reservations are only usually necessary in resort restaurants and the more exclusive independent establishments, although bookings are recommended in high season and during public holidays. Credit cards are accepted at most restaurants, but street vendors and some smaller establishments only accept cash.

WHERE TO EAT

Eating is a huge part of everyday life, with locals loving to snack all day long, whatever they are doing. Street stalls are open from early morning to late at night, serving dishes from *joke* (rice porridge), through to *kway teow naam moo* (pork noodle soup) and *satay gai* (chicken satay), ensuring there is something to eat at any given hour. The minimal cost means the street stalls and *raan aharn* (food shops) are always busy with people eating. Many snacks are available on sticks or bags should you want to eat 'on the go'.

Larger meals such as dinner are nearly always enjoyed with family or friends, when a selection of dishes is placed in the centre of the table for the group to share. Chopsticks are only used for noodle dishes, for everything else it's a fork and spoon. The meal will usually have at least a salad, soup or curry and a milder vegetable dish, accompanied by steamed rice, and there will often be a plate of raw green vegetables, such as cucumber, runner beans and maybe even raw cabbage at the centre of the table, which is a good cooling contrast with spicier items.

Food courts and street vendors, in particular, have a host of condiments to season dishes. Spring rolls, barbecued chicken and *goong sarong* (deep-fried prawns wrapped in vermicelli noodles) are accompanied by sweet chilli sauce. Fried rice comes with a small bowl of *naam prik pla* (fish sauce with chopped raw chilli), and when ordering noodles you almost always get four bowls containing fresh chillies in vinegar, dried chilli, fish sauce and sugar. A popular sauce with rice or noodles, and sometimes served with barbecued fish or meat dishes, is *naam prik phao*, a mixture of chillies, shallots, garlic and dried shrimp, roasted and then stir-fried with palm sugar, fish sauce and salt.

Cookery courses

Thai cookery courses run from a half-day to a full weekend. Most begin with a visit to a local market to select fresh foods, followed by a guided demonstration on how to prepare and cook some of the more common dishes.

WHAT TO EAT

Appetisers and salads

Som tam is the star of the salad spectrum, eaten widely all over the country. It's a refreshing, spicy-sour combination of shredded green papaya, garlic, chillies, lime juice, and variations of tomatoes, dried shrimp, preserved crab and fermented fish. Also look for *yam talay* (spicy seafood salad) or another sour-hot favourite *laab moo* (minced pork salad, made of minced meat, chilli, lime and roasted ground rice, also commonly served with beef and chicken). Snacky starters include the classic *po pia tod* (spring rolls) or *tod man pla* (Thai fish cakes) – both are served with a selection of sweet sauces.

Soup

Soups can be served as an appetiser, or as part of a main meal accompanied by rice. The well-known *tom yum goong* is a spicy and sour broth flavoured with chillies, lemongrass, kaffir lime and galangal, a root similar in taste to ginger. Another classic, *tom kha*, is milder, with a base of coconut milk for a softer, sweeter taste, and usually made with chicken *(gai)*.

Excellent seafood

Phuket has seafood restaurants on just about every street corner. Crabs, mussels, prawns, squid, red and white snapper and even shark are just a few of the specialities found in most restaurants. The unique 'Phuket lobster', which is recognisable by its large size, looks overwhelming, but you may still wish to tackle it, especially since the price of this delicacy is much lower than lobster in the Western world. Many restaurants allow their customers to select their own fish and seafood, and offer a variety of cooking options, including barbecuing, steaming or frying.

Both can be served with seafood, whole prawns or chicken.

Rice and noodles

Rice is most commonly steamed or boiled and served as an accompaniment to a main meal, but the popular fried rice, *kao pad*, can be ordered with chicken, pork, seafood or just vegetables, and is often a one-plate meal in itself. Like many Thai dishes, it comes with a cucumber, spring onion and lime garnish.

Sunday brunch at the Indigo Pearl Resort

The ubiquitous street-side noodle shop sells two types of noodle: *kuay tiaw*, made from rice flour, and *ba mee*, from wheat flour. Both can be ordered broad (*sen yai*), narrow (*sen lek*) or very narrow (*sen mee*), and with broth (*sai naam*) or without (*haeng*). *Pad thai* is a dry noodle dish stir-fried with bean sprouts, vegetables, meat, tamarind juice, lime, basil, garlic and onion. Also popular is *kway teow raat naa*, a combination of long, flat noodles stir-fried with vegetables, meat or seafood and a brown oyster sauce.

Seafood

Seafood is everywhere in the coastal south, with popular options including *pla muek tod kra tiem prik thai* (fried squid with garlic and pepper). *Pla ka pong neaung manow* translates

Seafood restaurant in Patong

as steamed whole fish with lemon, garlic and chilli, and *nor mai fa rung phad goong* is fried asparagus with shrimp. For something a little different, the soufflé-like *hor mok talay* is steamed, mildly spicy seafood served in banana-leaf bowls.

Chicken and meat

The best quality meats to order in traditional Thai eateries are chicken and pork. Beef is mainly used finely sliced in salads. Among the most popular meat dishes are green curry with chicken (*gaeng keow wan gai*), stir-fried chicken with cashew nuts (*gai phad med ma muang himaphaan*) and deep-fried pork rib with garlic and pepper (*see krong moo tod kra tiem prik thai*).

Sweets

A visit to Thailand would not be complete without sampling the delicious *kao noew ma-muang* (sticky rice and mango). This refreshing but very filling dessert combines fresh chopped

mango sprinkled with sesame seeds served over a bed of gluti-
nous sticky rice sweetened with sugar and coconut milk.

Fruit

Thais love fruit. It is commonly served for breakfast, with
lunch or after dinner, and is always available fresh from vendors along the beachfront, around town and in the markets.
Perhaps the most intriguing is the durian. Large, green and
covered in blunt spikes, it's hard to miss, but is often smelt
before it is seen. It's called the 'King of Fruit' and has an
odour most often compared to used toilets – the reason for
it being banned in many hotels. A polariser – people either
love or hate it – the durian's flesh is creamy, sweet and leaves
a heating sensation in the mouth. The 'Queen of Fruit' is the
small, purple, velvety-fleshed mangosteen. Also widely seen are
pineapple, watermelon, papaya, mango, coconut, banana and
rambutans *(ngor)*, which are red with soft spikes and a centre
similar to a lychee.

Thai rice

Although rice cultivation began in China, 4,000-year-old pottery shards
discovered in northeast Thailand show cultivation here was among the
earliest in history. Today Thailand is the world's largest rice exporter.
Thai jasmine rice, regularly stated to be the world's most fragrant, is
regarded as so valuable that the government patented its DNA. Even
the plain steamed or boiled rice seen at virtually every meal has the
affectionate name *khao suay* (beautiful rice). Particularly in the past, but
even now in rural areas, people will eat large helpings of rice with just
small portions of chilli, curry or sauce or morsels of dried or salted fish.
Of course, they might also enjoy more extravagant dishes like pineap-
ple-baked rice *(kao obb sapparot)* encased in a whole pineapple with
curried meat or seafood.

WHAT TO DRINK

Water, or *naam*, is essential to keep hydrated in the Thai heat. Tap water is not suitable for drinking, but bottled water is cheap and freely available. Avoid ice that comes in shavings, bits or large chunks, as it may not be fresh, but ice cubes in the majority of hotels and restaurants are safe.

Fruit shakes are freshly made and sold virtually everywhere. Among the most popular are banana shakes, and the less filling and arguably more refreshing watermelon or pineapple shake. Alternatively, it has been claimed that coconut water is full of electrolytes, which can help with rehydration after a spell in the sun.

A tropical fruit drink

As for alcohol, Phuket Beer is manufactured but rarely seen. Other local beers include Chang, Singha and Tiger, and a few places around the island stock Beer Lao. Heineken is also common, and is the best-known international brand available. All are sold in bottles rather than draught, except in a few of the larger, international pubs and bars. Some of the Irish bars serve Guinness, although it is usually more expensive than most other drinks.

Cocktails are popular, and most bars have extensive lists, although the quality and taste can vary dramatically from one outlet to another. For visual effect, order one of the cocktails served in a whole pineapple, which are available mainly along the open-air bars by the beaches. Local whiskies are inexpensive, popular and a lot more potent than they taste. Brands such as Mekhong and Sang Som are served with cola and ice, or in a bucket with a mixture of cola and Red Bull – guaranteed to keep you awake for hours.

Wine in Thailand is subject to heavy import charges and is more expensive than beer or spirits. At the airport, leave the duty-free spirits on the shelves – they are cheaper to buy once in the country – and instead bring a bottle of wine if that's what you prefer.

TO HELP YOU ORDER...

Do you have ...?	**Mee ... mai?**
I eat only vegetarian food	**Pom (male)/Dichan (female) kin jeh**
Not spicy	**Mai phet**
I can eat spicy food	**Pom/Dichan kin phet dai**
The bill, please	**Kep taang duay**
Could we have a table?	**Khaw toh dai mai?**
I'd like a/an/some ...	**Khaw ...**

beer	**bia**	ice	**naam khaeng**
cup	**thuay**	iced coffee	**kaa-fae yen**
fork	**sawm**	iced tea	**chaa yen**
fruit	**phon-la-mai**	menu	**meh-noo**
glass	**kaew**	spoon	**chawn**
hot coffee	**kaa-fae rawn**	steamed rice	**khao suay**
hot tea	**chaa rawn**	water	**naam**

...AND READ THE MENU

gaeng keow wan gai	green curry with chicken
gaeng phed gai/neua	red curry with chicken/beef

gai pad bai ka-phrao	chicken stir-fried with hot chillies and basil
gai pad khing	chicken stir-fried with ginger and mild chillies
gai pad med ma muang himaphaan	chicken stir-fried with dried chillies and cashews
gai thawt	fried chicken
gai yaang	grilled chicken
khai dao	fried egg
khai jiao	Thai-style omelette
kao pad gai/moo	fried rice with chicken/pork
kao tom moo/goong	rice soup with pork/prawns
kluay thawt	batter-fried bananas
kway teow pad see-yu	stir-fried rice noodles with soy sauce
goong phao	grilled prawns
moo krawp	crisp-fried pork
moo yaang	grilled pork
naam kluay pan	banana shake
naam taeng-moh pan	watermelon shake
pad phak	stir-fried vegetables
pad phak buay leng	stir-fried Chinese spinach
pad phak bung fai daeng	water spinach stir-fried with chillies, garlic and soy sauce
pad thai	rice noodles stir-fried with tofu, bean sprouts, egg, dried shrimp
prik naam pla	chillies in fish sauce
som tam	spicy green papaya salad
tom kha gai	galangal and coconut soup with chicken
tom yum goong	spicy lemongrass soup and prawns
yam pla duk foo	'exploded' catfish salad
yam pla muek	spicy squid salad

PLACES TO EAT

The following prices are for a three-course meal, excluding drinks, service and tax. At places with no service charge tips are discretionary.

$$$$** over 1,500 baht   **$$$ 750–1,500 baht
$$** 300–750 baht   **$ below 300 baht

PATONG

Baan Rim Pa $$$ *223 Prabaramee Road; tel: 0 7634 0789.* One of Phuket's most exclusive Thai restaurants is perched above a jagged rock face and boasts dramatic views of the sea below. The food here is of unbeatable quality, and is based around the less spicy 'Royal Thai' style of cuisine. A speciality of the house is the *goong sarong* – deep-fried prawns encased in crispy vermicelli noodles, which are freshly prepared and individually wrapped every morning. Open daily noon–midnight.

Baluchi $$ *Horizon Beach Resort, Soi Kep Sap; tel: 0 7629 2526; www.horizonbeach.com.* This restaurant serves authentic North Indian and a few Thai and international dishes. Set menus are available for lunch and dinner, as well as an extensive à la carte selection. Mutton *rogangosh* is the house speciality, although the tandoori *nisa* (barbecued tiger prawns) is also very impressive. Open daily lunch and dinner.

Da Maurizio $$$$ *223/2 Prabaramee Road; tel: 0 7634 4079; www.damaurizio.com.* One of the finest of Phuket's restaurants has waves breaking on rocks close to tables and flickering candlelight bouncing off the interior walls. While the delicious, beautifully presented food is mainly Italian, the menu also has surprises like grilled yellow tuna with harissa glaze and Moroccan couscous. Advance bookings are essential. Open daily noon–midnight.

Royale Nam Tok $$$$ *Soi Nam Tok, 116/102 Kathu, Patong Beach; tel: 08 7263 7327; www.royalenamtok.com.* Run by a Belgian couple, this posh traditional French restaurant is near a waterfall ten minutes' drive from Patong Beach. All the classics are here, from lobster bisque, through pan-fried foie gras de Strasbourg, to steak tartare. The interior is rococo, so has a French feel, or you can dine outside by the pool. Open Mon–Sat 6pm–9.30pm.

Sala Bua $$$ *Impiana Resort, 41 Thaweewong Road; tel: 0 7634 0138; www.impiana.com.my.* You can dine indoors or out at Patong's only true beachfront restaurant, where chef Dirk Schroeter presents a Mediterranean menu with Asian touches. Dishes such as foie gras with a Thai mango glaze and tea-smoked salmon are inventive and the desserts are very good. Open daily 6.30pm–midnight.

Savoey Seafood $$ *136 Thaweewong Road; tel: 0 7634 1171; www.savoeyseafood.com.* Select your meal from freshly caught daily offerings at the front of the restaurant. Try the whole snapper, either barbecued or steamed with a choice of sauces. The fried squid with garlic and pepper is also recommended. Meat dishes are available for those who are not keen on seafood. Open daily for lunch and dinner.

KARON

El Gaucho $$ *Movenpick Resort & Spa, 509 Patak Road; tel: 0 7639 6139; www.moevenpick-hotels.com.* This split-level restaurant with an outdoor terrace serves Brazilian-style churrasco grill, in which waiters tour the tables with various meats on skewers. You choose what you want and eat till you drop. Visits to the salad bar are included. Open daily 6pm–11pm.

Ging Restaurant $$ *192/36 Karon Road; tel: 08 1271 2446.* This well-run place is very busy, mainly for its friendly service and good Thai food, although it also has some Western choices. The menu runs the full gamut of local specialities like pepper garlic duck and *massaman* curry. Finish with ice cream. There is also free Wi-fi. Open daily for lunch and dinner.

Las Margaritas $$ *Phuket Hotel & Cantina, 528/7 Patak Road; tel: 0 7639 8350; www.las-margaritas.net.* Here you'll find a mix of cuisines from far across the globe, including Mexico, India, Hawaii, the Mediterranean and, of course, Thailand. Of the extensive selection of dishes, the Mexican offerings are the best. The sizzling chicken fajitas go down well with a bottle of Corona. Open daily for lunch and dinner.

On The Rock $$ *Marina Phuket Resort, 47 Karon Road; tel: 0 7633 0043; www.marinaphuket.com.* Cosy little restaurant within the Marina Phuket Resort, aptly named after the sea-facing rocks on which its elevated deck rests. The menu is predominantly Thai with a few Western dishes. Reservations are recommended. Open daily breakfast, lunch and dinner.

Ruam Thep $ *120/4 Moo 2, Patak Road West.* A cunningly hidden Thai and seafood restaurant on the cosy southern corner of Hat Karon. Service is friendly, and the menu is large enough to justify sipping on one of the popular fresh banana milkshakes as you read through it. Although unassuming in appearance, the food at this little restaurant is fantastic. Open daily for lunch and dinner.

KATA

Boathouse Wine and Grill $$$$ *182 Kata Road; tel: 0 7633 0015; www.boathousephuket.com.* This romantic beach-facing restaurant is home to one of Phuket's most extensive wine lists and has 24 labels available by the glass. Choose from air-conditioned indoor tables or alfresco decking just metres from the waves. The ambience is casual yet upmarket, with both French and Thai degustation menus available. The former has dishes like lamb loin with green asparagus, mushrooms, celery mash and vegetable tian, and the latter poached sea bass fillet with lemongrass, chilli, lime juice and kaffir lime leaves. Open daily for lunch and dinner.

Capannina $$ *30/9 Moo 2, Kata Road; tel: 0 7628 4318; www.capannina-phuket.com.* Popular restaurant with wood-fired ovens, offering authentic dishes from across the various regions of Italy. Warm and welcoming mustard and terracotta walls and a mix of open-air tables and covered cushions create a cosy dining atmosphere. Beware of the large pizza – measuring a whopping 60cm (23in) in diameter, it often requires a table of its own. Open daily noon–11pm.

Kata Mama $ *South end of Hat Kata Yai; tel: 0 7628 4301.* This popular family-run operation serving home-style Thai dishes and seafood has been around for over 35 years. It offers favourites such as fried fish with garlic and pepper, and barbecued prawns with chilli sauce. The beachfront location is a pull, too. Open daily 8am–midnight.

Mali Seafood $$$ *Sugar Palm Resort, 20/10 Kata Road; tel: 0 7628 4404; www.sugarpalmphuket.com.* Meaning 'jasmine' in Thai, this informal, open-sided, 100-seater eatery serves a menu of international and Thai food in a decor of pine floors and an off-white colour scheme. A soundtrack of frothy Top 40s music accompanies signature dishes like grilled grouper with mango salsa. Open daily for breakfast, lunch and dinner.

KAMALA

Rockfish $$$–$$$$ *33/6 Kamala Beach Road; tel: 0 7627 9732; www.rockfishrestaurant.com.* Rockfish has a beautiful elevated cliffside location with panoramic views out towards the bay. Minimalist tables sit on wooden decking, subtly lit to create a chic ambience. The menu is a mix of Thai and Western specialities, with tempting modern offerings such as chilli-marinated tuna with fresh coconut juice; goat's cheese fritter with red onion marmalade; and roasted scallops, chorizo and spring onion with slow-roast tomato risotto. Open daily 8am–late.

Silk Bar and Restaurant $$$ *15 Moo 6, Kamala Beach; tel: 0 7633 8777; www.silkphuket.com.* This chic and trendy eatery has a modern approach to Thai food, both in its funky presentation and its techniques. Dishes include chicken poached in coconut milk with lemongrass. The stylish interior generates a relaxed mood, with sleek deck-style furniture, lots of teak and tubular Thai-silk lampshades. Large windows overlook a pool, where you can also dine. Open daily for lunch and dinner.

SURIN

Catch Beach Club $$$ *Surin Beach Road, Choeng Thale; tel: 0 7631 6567; www.catchbeachclub.com.* An alfresco eatery with indoor tables and a long bar, as well as bamboo tables set directly on the sand to create a very elegant and tropical feel. Seafood is the house speciality, with fresh catches offered up daily, but there's also a wide choice of international food, with daily lunch and dinner buffets as well as à la carte. Weekend bookings are advised. Open daily for lunch and dinner.

BANG TAO

360 Degrees $$$ *31/1 Moo 6, Choeng Thale; tel: 0 7631 7600; www.thepavilionsresorts.com.* Part of the luxury Phuket Pavilions resort, this smart, timber-floored, hilltop restaurant is in a romantic spot with gorgeous sunsets. It bills its well-presented fare as 'gourmet café food' and it delivers in dishes like tuna with ginger, chilli and coriander, smoked pork back ribs and dark chocolate fondue. Open daily for dinner.

The Red Room $$–$$$ *293/25-26 Srisoonthorn Road; tel: 0 7627 1136; www.theresidenceresort.com.* The clean lines and red walls create a serene ambience at this restaurant owned by, but separate from, the Residence Resort. Eat inside or out from a straightforward Thai and European menu, with items ranging from *tom yum goong* to lobster bisque, and from red curry to rack of lamb. Open daily for breakfast, lunch and dinner.

The Siam Supper Club $$$ *36-40 Lagoon Road; tel: 0 7627 0936; www.siamsupperclub.com.* There's a chic but informal ambiance here, with lounge sounds and well-prepared international cuisine. Goat's-cheese salad, pastas and mouth-watering meat dishes, including grilled Australian beef tenderloin and herb-coated rack of lamb, are typical. Open daily 6pm–1am.

PHUKET TOWN

The Blue Elephant $$$–$$$$ *96 Krabi Road; tel 0 7635 4355; www.blueelephant.com.* In the glorious former governor's mansion, this worldwide chain presents Thai food with foreigner-friendly flavours. It's mainly traditional but with some successful interchange of product and technique in dishes such as salmon *laab* and medium-rare seared duck breast with sweet tamarind sauce. It also offers cooking lessons. Open daily for lunch and dinner.

Natural Restaurant $ *62/5 Soi Phutorn; tel: 0 7622 4287.* The interior at this pleasing, multi-level Thai restaurant sits somewhere between junk shop and garden centre. Plants and trees grow between a collection that includes birdcages, bicycles, toys and TV-screen aquariums. The delicious food includes stir-fried kale with salted fish, green curry and coconut steamed fish in pandanus leaves. It's an excellent place for large groups to gather and enjoy a fabulous meal at very reasonable prices. Open daily 10.30am–11.30pm.

Salvatore's $$–$$$ *15 Rassada Road; tel: 0 7622 5958; www.salvatorestaurant.com.* The portly Salvatore oversees this generous Italian menu that starts with appetisers like lobster Catalan style and moves through pastas and risotto to main courses. Try gnocchi with lamb sauce, followed by home-made ice cream, and round off with fresh ground Italian coffee. The tables in its rustic interior are fully booked most nights so reservations are strongly recommended. Open Tue–Sat for lunch and dinner, Sun for dinner.

Siam Indigo Exotique Bar and Restaurant $$ *8 Phang Nga Road; tel: 0 7625 6697; www.siamindigo.com.* This French-owned eatery is in an 80-year-old building. It features tall windows and thick-beamed ceilings, and is captivatingly decorated with colourful local art pieces contrasted against crisp, white furniture. The menu features exquisite Thai dishes using the freshest ingredients selected that day, although the staff are pleased to discuss other styles if you don't fancy Thai. Be sure to save space for dessert – the patisserie-style baked selections are outstanding – but for sheer indulgence it is hard to beat the white chocolate mousse. Open daily Wed–Mon for lunch and dinner.

Tung-Ka Café $$ *Rang Hill, Korsimbee Road; tel: 0 7621 1500.* Perhaps the restaurant with the best view of Phuket Town, Tung-Ka Café is halfway up the winding Rang Hill, where it has been serving Thai cuisine for over 30 years. Lunchtimes are less busy, but the view in the evening is far more impressive. All dishes are good, and the *penang* curry is particularly worth trying. Be sure to specify if you want it without excess chillies. Open daily 11am–11pm.

CHALONG

Kan Eang $$ *44/1 Viset Road; tel: 0 7638 1323.* A large yet intimate open-air, pier-side restaurant with tiny fairy lights dotted in the trees and well-spaced wooden tables lit in the evenings by simple candlelight. It's a peaceful location where small boats bob in the waters as diners tuck into mostly seafood dishes, either barbecued or steamed and accompanied with a variety of sauces. Open daily 10am–10pm.

Viset Restaurant $$$ *44/1 Viset Road; tel: 0 7638 1159.* This semi open-air restaurant at Chalong Pier has chic café decor with smart wooden tables, perspex chairs and an open kitchen. The 'modern Western' menu has high-end products like foie gras and Wagyu beef and neat touches such as red snapper with quail-egg salad. Open daily 11.30am–11pm.

RAWAI/NAI HARN

Nikita's $$ *44/1 Rawai Beach Road; tel: 0 7628 8703; www.nikitas-phuket.com.* Directly on Rawai Beach, Nikita's is a beautiful location for a quiet Sunday afternoon. The menu is predominantly Thai, and although there is a strong emphasis on seafood, the meat dishes are equally tasty. The restaurant also serves a few Western dishes like burgers and pizzas, along with draught cider and a few imported beers. Views are of fishing boats bobbing near the cluster of islands beyond, and the ambience is one of relaxation and tranquillity. Open daily from 10am until late.

L'Orfeo $$–$$$ *95/13 Moo 7, Soi Saiyuan; tel: 0 7628 8935; www.orfeo-phuket.com.* This is a wonderfully romantic spot if you can get a table. Tuna tartare with plum and ginger, and lamb tenderloin are good choices. Desserts change regularly, but keep an eye out for the home-made lemon tart. Open daily for dinner (high season), Mon–Sat for dinner (low season); closed Sept and Oct.

A–Z TRAVEL TIPS

A Summary of Practical Information

A

ACCOMMODATION

The type of budget, backpacker-style accommodation found elsewhere in Thailand is not so evident in Phuket. There are some small guesthouses, but these are typically confined to the town centre. Most of the accommodation along the beaches is in hotels, ranging from moderately priced to luxury and even exclusive villas. Another option is to rent a serviced apartment. One bedroom places start around 1,500 baht a night at www.sabaai.com, and cheaper by the week or month.

As a rule of thumb, accommodation in the south of the island is cheaper than elsewhere. There are a few high-end resorts, but much of the accommodation is pretty basic and is above or next to bars or dive shops. It is often comfortable and sufficient if only intended for use as a base, but do not expect any frills. The north of the island, by contrast, is turning increasingly upmarket, with luxurious spa resorts and private villas for rent. The most popular beaches of Patong, Karon and Kata on the west coast are more central, and accommodation here generally falls between the two price extremes.

Rates vary dramatically between high season and low season. Check for hidden costs if staying on the island on Christmas Eve, New Year's Eve, and over the Chinese New Year, as virtually all hotels and many guesthouses hold compulsory 'gala' dinners, for which each guest must purchase a ticket.

single room	**hawng diaw**
double room	**hawng khoo**
I'd like a single/double room with bathroom.	**Tawng-kaan hawng diaw/ khoo hawng naam nai tua.**
What's the rate per night?	**Khaa hawng thao rai?**

The majority of hotels charge a 10 percent service charge and 7 percent VAT on top of the room rate. These charges are often not included in the published price.

AIRPORT

Phuket International Airport (HKT; tel: 0 7632 7230; www.airport thai.co.th) is small and under increasing pressure from expanding markets. Planned airport expansions won't be operational until 2015.

Some airlines offer direct international flights from Australia and Asia, but those from the UK and Continental Europe stop in Bangkok, from where a number of airlines operate reasonably priced daily domestic flights to Phuket. These include **Thai Airways** (www.thaiair.com), **Nok Air** (www.nokair.com), **Bangkok Airways** (www.bangkokair.com) and **Thai Air Asia** (www.airasia.com).

International flights to Bangkok land at Suvarnabhumi Airport, while domestic flights from Bangkok increasingly operate from the older Dong Muang Airport. Travel time between the two airports varies depending on Bangkok's notoriously congested traffic conditions, but it is advisable to allow at least an hour to get from one to the other.

I need a taxi.	**Tawng-kaan rot taek-see.**
How much is it to...?	**Bai... thao rai?**
Does this bus go to...?	**Rot meh nee bai... mai?**

Flight time from Bangkok to Phuket is approximately one hour and 10 minutes. Expect particularly long queues if clearing immigration in Phuket during peak seasons. There are few shops and restaurants in the arrival hall.

The airport is located 28km north of Phuket Town. Metered red-and-yellow taxis take around 30 minutes, with fares costing approximately 350 baht. Buses to Phuket Town are every 30 minutes from 8.20am–7.50pm and make several stops on the way. Tickets are 90 baht for the full one-hour journey.

B

BICYCLE AND MOTORCYCLE HIRE

Cycling is not popular in Phuket, as most people feel safer on the roads in either a car or motorcycle, despite motorcycle accidents being very common. There are, however, a number of viewpoints that can be cycled around, and tour operators should also be able to advise on areas away from the main roads. If you wish to cycle, contact your hotel reception or a tour operator for details. Motorcycles can be rented at hotels, restaurants, guesthouses, bars and travel agents across the island.

BUDGETING FOR YOUR TRIP

Phuket is inexpensive compared with most Western destinations, but it is slightly more expensive than elsewhere in Thailand. It is possible to eat well on around 500 baht per day, although you could also get by on a lot less. At the time of writing, there were approximately 50 baht to the pound and 30 baht to the US dollar.

Transport: Taxi or tuk-tuk: 200–600 baht per trip. Motorcycle taxi: 50–200 baht per trip. Average fare of a domestic one-way flight: 2,000 baht.

Meals: Dining in even the cheaper hotels is generally a lot more expensive than eating at the local restaurants. On average, breakfast and lunch will cost around 150–250 baht at restaurants, and double this within hotels. Expect to pay 200–500 baht for a reasonable dinner. Dining at the island's top restaurants is more expensive, often even by Western standards, mainly due to the heavy wine prices caused by high import taxes. Main courses at these places will cost between 600 and 1,000 baht. Generally soft drinks, spirits and beer are relatively cheap. When shopping anywhere outside the large malls it is always worth asking for a discount, which should kickstart a bargaining process.

C

CAMPING

Camping is permitted on certain beaches within Sirinat National Park in the northwest of Phuket. Tents can be rented from the visitor centre on the southern end of Mai Khao Beach, and there are a few basic bungalows on Nai Yang Beach. Contact the National Park Authority for details (tel: 0 7632 7407; www.dnp.go.th).

CAR AND MOTORBIKE HIRE

Rental prices for a standard car range from around 700 to 2,500 baht per day (and can be more in peak season).

Motorcycles are a lot cheaper (and a lot more dangerous); a 125cc bike can be hired for as little as 200 baht for the whole day. Be sure to double-check insurance details, as many of the less reputable companies do not have adequate cover.

Lack of insurance, along with failure to wear a helmet, are the most common reasons for intervention from traffic police, who generally impose an on-the-spot fine.

When hiring a vehicle, always opt for the full insurance package, especially the Collision Damage Waiver (CDW). Although some credit-card companies cover this, you would have to produce an enormous amount of paperwork, which would be difficult and costly to translate from Thai.

Budget tel: 0 7620 5396; www.budget.co.th
Phuket Car Rent tel: 0 7620 5190; www.phuketcarrent.com

I'd like to rent a car	**Yak ja chao rot yon**
tomorrow	**wan phrung nee**
for one day/	**neung wan/**
week	**neung aathit**
with full insurance.	**phrawm prakan rot.**

CLIMATE

Phuket's tropical climate means that the weather is warm year-round. Even in 'winter' (November to February) the temperature rarely drops much below 25°C (77°F). The best time to visit is between November and February, when humidity is low, it seldom rains, and the skies are sunny. March and April are usually still dry, but heat and humidity rise in the build-up to the May-to-late-October rainy season. The rainy season is often somewhat misunderstood, as despite the odd cluster of days where driving wind and rain prevail, the skies are generally clear, with heavy downpours only in the evening and at night. Seas at this time can be quite rough, and red flags signalling dangerous swimming conditions should be taken notice of.

Temperatures in the mid- to late 30s (95–100°F) are not uncommon in the March-to-April hot season, although air-conditioned buildings and sea breezes make this time of year more bearable here than in the capital, Bangkok.

CLOTHING

As the primary religion is Buddhism, it is courteous to cover up in restaurants and shops, and knees and shoulders should be covered if entering temples. Formal attire is practically unheard of in Phuket, and even most business people dress casually.

CRIME AND SAFETY

Beware of pickpockets in crowded marketplaces and packed bars and use common sense. If your hotel reception has an area in which valuables can be deposited; always obtain a receipt.

Call the police!	**Khaw jaeng tam-ruat!**
Help!	**Chuay duay!**
Call a doctor!	**Khaw riak maw!**
Danger!	**Antaraai!**

Street violence is uncommon and women are rarely victims of harassment. Prostitutes occasionally drug clients (sometimes fatally) and steal valuables. If you are a victim of crime it is easier in the first instance to call the Tourist Police (1155; www.tourist.police.go.th) as they speak English.

Drug use and the possession of drugs are taken very seriously in Thailand. The maximum penalty is life imprisonment or death.

D

DISABLED TRAVELLERS

Thailand falls short on accommodating people with disabilities, although top hotels will have better facilities. Getting to many of the smaller islands often entails taking boats moored at poorly designed piers. There are some online resources, such as www.disabledthailand.com.

DRIVING

Road conditions. All driving in Thailand is on the left. Overtake and give way to the right. Although not busy and congested like Bangkok, conditions on Phuket are still nothing short of chaotic. The flashing of headlights by an oncoming vehicle means that it is coming through regardless. The best way to drive is to assume that everyone that can get in your way, will – that way there are fewer surprises.

Although it is illegal, drink-driving is commonplace, and there are regular road accidents. Statistically, there is at least one fatal crash each week, with the majority involving motorcyclists.

Rules and regulations. An international driver's licence is required for visitors to Thailand. The official speed limit is 50km/h (30mph) in towns, 80km/h (50mph) on main roads and 120km/h (70mph) on highways.

Fuel. Service stations are plentiful, but many shut by 8pm.

Parking. Major shopping centres have covered parking, which gets more cramped at weekends. Parking bays are situated along most streets. In many cases, which side of the road you are permitted to park on will be determined by whether the date is an odd or even number. Look to signs for an indication.

If you need help. Telephone the agency from which you rented the car to come and help you. In an emergency, dial the tourist police (tel: 1155; www.tourist.police.go.th).

Road signs. Major roads are signposted in English. Beware of contradictory road signs. Often a 'No U-turn' sign will be placed immediately in front of a sign telling you U-turns are permissible. A blue sign with a white arrow pointing to the left or right at a junction indicates that if conditions are safe you can ignore the traffic lights and turn on the red light.

accident	**u-bat-fi-het**
collision	**rot chon**
fill (the petrol tank)	**dem**
flat tyre	**yang baen**
Help!	**Chuay duay!**
Police!	**Tam ruat!**
Slow down!	**Cha-cha!**

E

ELECTRICITY

The standard current in Thailand is 220-volt, 50-cycle AC; most hotel rooms have an electrical outlet for shavers; some also have 110-volt sockets. Plugs are two-pin, and you'll need adaptors (and transformers, depending on where you're coming from).

EMBASSIES

All embassies are located in Bangkok:
Australia: 37 Satorn Tai Road; tel: 0 2344 6300; www.thailand.embassy.gov.au.

Canada: 990 Rama IV Road, Abdulrahim Place, 15th Floor; tel: 0 2636 0540; www.canadainternational.gc.ca.

Ireland: 4th Fl, Room 407, Thaniya Building, 62 Silom Road; tel: 0 2632 6720; www.irelandinthailand.com.

New Zealand: M Thai Tower, 14th Fl, All Seasons Place, 87 Wireless Road; tel: 0 2254 2530; www.nzembassy.com.

South Africa: 12th Fl, M Thai Tower, All Seasons Place, 87 Wireless Road; tel: 0 2659 2900; www.saembbangkok.com.

UK: 14 Wireless Road, tel: 0 2305 8333; ukinthailand.fco.gov.uk.

US: 120–122 Wireless Road; tel: 0 2205 4000; www.bangkok.us embassy.gov.

The US and UK have occasional visiting consular clinics and some countries have consular representatives in Phuket with the following contacts:

Australia: tel: 0 7637 2600

Ireland: tel: 0 7628 1273; www.consulateirelandphuket.org.

embassy	**sathaan thoot**
passport	**nang seu doen thaang**
visa	**wee-saa**
Where's the British/ American embassy?	**Sathaan thoo angkrit/ amerikaa yoo thee nai?**

EMERGENCIES

In case of emergency it is best to contact the tourist police on 1155, who will speak English. The regular emergency number is 191.

G

GAY AND LESBIAN TRAVELLERS

Although the gay scene is quieter than Bangkok, there are several gay-owned establishments in Phuket Town and Patong, including bars, restaurants and small hotels. Most of the action takes place around the Paradise Complex on Rat Utit Road in Patong, and there is an annual gay festival in April. Gay Patong (www.gaypatong.com) is a good resource for local information.

Purple Dragon (www.purpledrag.com) is a highly respected gay and lesbian travel company, and there's more about Thailand and the region at Utopia (www.utopia–asia.com).

GETTING TO PHUKET

By air. The island's international airport receives daily non-stop flights from Australia, Malaysia, Hong Kong and Singapore. There are no non-stop scheduled flights from London. Most people fly to Bangkok on carriers such as British Airways (www.britishairways.com), Eva Air (www.evaair.com) or Thai (www.thaiairways.com) and then take a domestic connection through airlines such as Air Asia (www.airasia.com) and Bangkok Airways (www.bangkokair.com). The flight time to Bangkok from London is around 12 hours. From Bangkok to Phuket is 1hr 10 minutes. Non-stop airlines from Australia include Virgin Australia (www.virginaustralia.com).

Domestic flights from Bangkok leave daily from Suvarnabhumi Airport or Don Muang Airport. Check the internet for the best deals.

By bus. The rise of budget airlines has seen a fall in the demand for coach travel, but buses leave Bangkok's Southern Bus Terminal nightly for the 14-hour trip. Regional buses now operate from Phuket Bus Terminal 2 on Thepkrasattri Road, Rassada, which opened in 2012. It has departure points for fixed-price taxis and motorcycles to carry arrivals to other points on the island.

By boat. Foot passengers from Krabi and Ko Phi Phi are dropped at Rassada Pier in Phuket Town. The journey from each place can take anywhere from two to three hours, depending on the weather and sea conditions. Boats from Ko Lanta travel via Krabi or Ko Phi Phi, although they often do not run between May and October due to bad weather.

GUIDES AND TOURS

A list of licensed English-speaking guides can be obtained from the Tourism Authority of Thailand (TAT). By law these guides are required to wear their official photo identification card around their neck at all times.

Often a guide will come with a driver, particularly on group tours. Hotel receptions can give an indication of the approximate rates that would be considered reasonable. It is customary to provide lunch or invite the guide to eat with you, particularly on full-day trips. Alternatively, you may tip the guide and driver at the end of the day to cover the cost of lunch.

Siam Safari (tel: 0 7628 0116; www.siamsafari.com) is a respected operator for land-based excursions incorporating jeep safaris, elephant trekking, canoeing and visits to Thai villages and national parks. And on water, Island Divers (tel: 0 7560 1082; www.island-diverspp.com) on Ko Phi Phi organises day trips and live-aboard diving, as well as snorkelling and kayaking tours.

H

HEALTH AND MEDICAL CARE

No vaccinations are required to enter Thailand, but check with your doctor before you travel whether any vaccinations or other medical precautions are advised. During the rainy season you should spray repellent to deter the mosquito that carries dengue fever. Infection is not common, but if you begin to exhibit severe flu-like symptoms, contact a doctor immediately.

Tap water is not safe to drink. Bottled water is cheap and readily available everywhere. Ice in drinks is generally safe in reputable restaurants and hotels. Avoid ice that comes in shavings, bits or large chunks.

Over-indulgence in rich or spicy foods, and too much sun, are as common a cause of stomach disorders as actual bugs. Experiment with new foods gradually and avoid becoming dehydrated.

Local health clinics often only take cash, but credit cards are accepted in all major hospitals. Thailand has no reciprocal agreements with foreign countries, so arrange health insurance before you leave. Hospitals are of an excellent standard, and there are 24-hour pharmacies across the island. The costs of medical treatment and supplies are significantly lower than in Western countries. Many medications that would usually require prescriptions back home can be dispensed freely over the counter.

a bottle of drinking water	**nam yen nung khuad**
I need a doctor.	**Pom (if male)/chan (if female) tong karn maw.**
I need a dentist.	**Pom/chan tong karn maw fan.**
pharmacy/	**raan khaai yaa/**
hospital/doctor	**rohng phayaabaan/maw**

L

LANGUAGE

English is widely used across Phuket, but it is useful to know some basic Thai phrases when in restaurants or shops. The language can be difficult, as it uses tones, and one word may have up to five different pronunciations and meanings. Certain tones are different in Phuket than Bangkok. There is no universal transliteration system from Thai into English, which is why street names can be spelled in three different ways, sometimes along the same street.

M

MAPS

Basic maps can be picked up free. More detailed maps can be found in bookshops. The 'Groovy Phuket Map' is one of the best.

MEDIA

The *Bangkok Post* and *The Nation* are Thailand's leading English-language newspapers. They are also online at www.bangkokpost.com and www.nationmultimedia.com.

The English-language weekly newspaper the *Phuket Gazette* (www.phuketgazette.com) can be bought at outlets across the island.

Thailand has five terrestrial television channels, which often show foreign programmes, although they will be dubbed into Thai.

MONEY

Currency. The unit of currency in Thailand is the baht (abbreviated to THB, Bt or B), which is divided into 100 satang. Banknotes come in denominations of 20, 50, 100, 500 and 1,000 baht. Coins are 25 and 50 satang, and 1, 2, 5 and 10 baht.

Banks and exchange facilities. Normally the exchange rate at banks is the most favourable. After the banks are closed you can change money at your hotel, at exchange booths or at shops displaying a sign in English saying 'moneychanger'. Banks and moneychangers in tourist towns will accept virtually any currency.

Credit cards. Major hotels, restaurants and shops are accustomed to credit cards. Small eateries and small shops tend to accept cash only.

Can I pay by credit card?	**Jaai pen bat credit yang nee dai mai?**
I want to change some pounds/dollars.	**Yaak ja laek plian pound/dollar.**
Can you cash a travellers' cheque?	**Laek plian chek doen thaang dai mai?**
Where's the nearest bank?	**Thanaakhaan klai-sut yoo thee nai?**
Is there a cash machine near here?	**Mee khreuang atm klai thee nee mai?**

O

OPENING TIMES

Business hours are 8.30am–noon and 1–4.30pm, Monday–Friday. Many offices also open for a half-day on Saturdays. Banks are open 8.30am–3.30pm. Central Festival shopping centre, outside Phuket Town, opens its doors at 9am, although only the food supermarkets are accessible before 11am. Jungceylon, in Patong, opens at 10am. Both shopping complexes close at 10pm.

State-run museums are closed on Monday and Tuesday.

All bars and establishments selling alcohol are required to close by 1am, but Phuket seems to be exempt from the rule, and generally there will always be somewhere to party until the early hours.

P

POLICE

Thai military police wear beige uniforms and white helmets with a red stripe. Those in tourist areas usually have passable English. Near the beaches are the tourist police, who wear a similar uniform to the military police but with a tourist police patch on the shoulder. Dial 1155 for the tourist police, who are generally more helpful in minor situations than the military police. The main police station is at 100/31-32 Chalem Prakiat Road, Phuket Town (tel: 0 7635 5015).

police	**tam-ruat**
tourist police	**tam-ruat thawng thiaw**
Where's the nearest police station?	**Sathaanee tam-ruat thee klai-sut yoo thee nai?**
I've lost my...	**... haai**
wallet/bag/ passport.	**kra-bao ngoen/kra-bao/ nang seu doen thaang.**

POST OFFICES

Phuket's main post office is on Montri Road in Phuket Town, with additional branches in Patong, Karon, Rawai and Thalang. Opening hours are 8.30am–4.30pm Monday–Friday and 9am–noon on Saturday.

Post should arrive at its destination within a week. Registered mail can be arranged at any post office. Post boxes are red and easily recognisable on the streets.

Where's the nearest post office?	**Praisanee klai-sut yoo thee nai?**
express (special delivery)	**EMS**
registered	**long tha-bian**

PUBLIC HOLIDAYS

During religious holidays and government elections, alcohol is often forbidden in bars, shops and restaurants.

1 January New Year's Day
6 April Chakri Day, honouring Rama I
13–15 April Songkran (Water Festival for Thai New Year)
1 May Labour Day
5 May Coronation Day
12 August Queen's Birthday
23 October Chulalongkorn Day, honouring Rama V
5 December King's Birthday and National Day
10 December Constitution Day
31 December New Year's Eve
Variable dates:
Chinese New Year (first month of the lunar calendar, usually Jan/Feb).
Maka Puja (full moon in February). Commemoration of the meeting at which the Buddha preached the doctrines of Buddhism.

Visakha Puja (full moon in May). Celebrates the birth, enlightenment and death of the Buddha. Most holy Buddhist ceremonial day.
Asanha Puja (full moon in July). Celebrates the Buddha's first sermon.
Vegetarian Festival (ninth month of the lunar calendar, usually mid- to late Oct).

T

TELEPHONES

Thailand's country code is 66. To make an overseas phone call from Thailand you must first dial 001, followed by the country code and area code without the initial zero. For international call assistance dial 100. Mobile phone numbers begin with 08.

Telephone services are provided at most hotels or at business centres and internet cafés around the island. Rates are posted in English. Prepaid international phonecards can be bought at post offices, but public telephones are not always the best option for long-distance calls due to noisy locations or bad connections.

Users of GSM 900 or 1800 mobile phones with an international roaming facility can hook up automatically to the local Thai network. Check with your service provider if you are not sure – and ask about costs. Alternatively, Thai SIM cards can be bought for a few hundred baht, with prepaid top-up cards widely available. Mobile phones can be bought second-hand for as little as 2,000 baht.

telephone	**thohrasaap**
long-distance call	**thohrasaap thaan klaai**
international call	**thohrasaap rawaang pratheht**
Can you get me this number?	**Khaw mai-lehk thohrasaap nee dai mai?**
reverse-charge (collect) call	**thohrasaap kep plaai thaang**

TIME ZONES

Thailand is seven hours ahead of GMT so when it's 7am in London it's 2pm in Phuket. Night falls between 6pm and 7pm year-round, so daylight-saving time is not observed.

In January:					
New York	London	Johannesburg	Phuket	Sydney	Auckland
00am	5am	7am	noon	4pm	6pm
In July:					
New York	London	Johannesburg	Phuket	Sydney	Auckland
1am	6am	7am	noon	3pm	5pm

TIPPING

Tipping is not generally a custom in Thailand, although restaurants (not small Thai places) and hotels will add a service charge of 10 percent to your bill. People leave loose change left over from their bill in cafés and taxis. Twenty baht is standard for porters in mid-range hotels. A 10 percent tip is customary for massage therapists.

TOILETS

Toilets in Phuket are generally cleaner than those in Bangkok, although you may still encounter squat toilets in some small restaurants or in local Thai areas, and certainly at bus or service stations if you venture off the island.

A helpful tip for women is to face away from the door, in the opposite manner as they would in a Western toilet. Squat toilets are flushed by pouring water from a large bucket or tank with a plastic scoop.

Where are the toilets?	**Hong nam yu tee nai?**

TOURIST INFORMATION

The Tourism Authority of Thailand (TAT, www.tourismthailand.org) operates information stands in the arrival hall at Phuket International Airport. The main TAT Office in Phuket is at Thalang Road, Phuket Town, open daily 8.30am–4.30pm, tel: 0 7621 2213, where you can obtain leaflets, maps and advice.

Overseas representatives of the Tourism Authority of Thailand can be found in the following countries:

Australia: Australia 2002, Level 20, 56 Pitt Street, Sydney; tel: 61-2-9247 7549; www.tourismthailand.org/au.

UK: 1st Floor, 17–19 Cockspur Street, Trafalgar Square, London; tel: 0-870-900 2007; www.tourismthailand.co.uk.

US: 611 North Larchmont Boulevard, Los Angeles, CA 90004; tel: 1-323-461 9814; 61 Broadway, suite 2810, New York, NY 10006; tel: 1-212-432 0433.

TRANSPORT

Public transport is plentiful around the tourist areas, beaches and shopping centres, but elsewhere on the island it is notoriously lacking. Taxis and tuk-tuks are significantly more expensive than in the rest of the country. Hop-on, hop-off bus services linking the airport with Kamala, Patong and Rawai may open in the near future.

Local buses. Small, blue public buses (*songthaew*) are infrequent and painfully slow but very cheap. They operate between the bus station in Phuket Town and the beaches for 30–40 baht, from 6am–6pm (return journeys end at 4pm). Residents in Phuket Town now also have the Po Thong pink bus network (tel: hotline 1131, 0 7621 0806), which runs around town from 6am–8pm, priced 10–20 baht per trip. Local buses go from the central bus terminal on Ranong Road in Phuket Town (tel: 0 3251 1230). Services depart half-hourly between 7am and 6pm to the various beaches, but no buses run from one beach to another. The airport bus (www.airportbusphuket.com) also terminates there. Phuket Bus Terminal 2 on Thepkrasattri Road, Rassada, serves inter-regional buses.

Motorcycle taxis. Although a cheap way to travel, motorcycle taxi are certainly more risky. They can be convenient for short trips, but are not advisable for longer journeys.

Taxis. Taxis in Phuket are not easily distinguishable from normal cars with a driver. In most places, they are few and far between, with the exception of the shopping centres, the airport and Phuket Bus Terminal 2, where taxi ranks display fixed rates for the main beaches. None are metered. They are mostly air-conditioned, and are more comfortable than tuk-tuks. Phuket Airport Taxi (tel: 0 7637 9571; www.phuketairporttaxi.com) is one of few companies that lets you book taxis by phone.

Tuk-tuks. Phuket tuk-tuks are four-wheeled, bright red and resemble a shrunken minivan. Tuk-tuks are not equipped with meters, and fares must be agreed before climbing aboard. Never agree to the initial asking price, and expect to pay more in bad weather or after midnight. Most drivers speak good English. You can hail tuktuks anywhere. Prices to beaches from Phuket Town should start at 300 baht.

boat	**reua**
bus	**rot meh**
taxi	**thaek-see**
Where can I get a taxi?	**Mee rot thaek-see thee nai?**
What's the fare to... ?	**Bai... raakhaa thao rai?**
Where is the bus stop?	**Rot meh klai-sut yoo thee nai?**
What time does the next bus to... leave?	**Rot pai... thiaw naa awk kee mohng?**
I want a ticket to...	**Yaak ja seu tua bai...**
single/return	**thiaw diaw/bai klap**
Will you tell me when to get off?	**Khaw bawk wehlaa theung laew?**

V

VISAS AND ENTRY REQUIREMENTS

All foreign nationals entering Thailand must have passports with at least six-month validity. Nationals from most countries, including the UK, Australia, Ireland, New Zealand, South Africa and the US, will be granted a visa on arrival valid for 30 days. For a full list see the Thai Ministry of Foreign Affairs website at www.mfa.go.th. To qualify for a visa you also need a return or onward ticket. Always check the latest requirements before you travel, as regulations can change.

Visas can be extended by 30 days for 1,000 baht in Bangkok or at the regional immigration offices (Phuket Road, tel: 0 7622 1905) or you can leave the country (even for half an hour) and return to receive another visa on entry. In total, tourists can stay in Thailand for a cumulative period not exceeding 90 days within any six-month period from the date of first entry.

Overstaying can carry a daily fine of 500 baht to a maximum of 20,000 baht on leaving the country, but if the police catch you before you try leaving you may face imprisonment.

W

WEBSITES, BLOGS AND INTERNET CAFÉS

A great source of information from someone who has lived in Phuket for years is Jamie Monk's blog at http://jamie-monk.blog spot.co.uk.

Internet cafés charge a standard rate of 1–3 baht per minute with a 10-minute minimum charge. Useful websites include:

www.langhub.com/en-th Audio and video files to learn Thai.
www.phuket.com Information guide and booking service.
www.phuketgazette.com Leading English-language newspaper.
www.phuket.net Information on all aspects of Phuket.
www.thaiairways.com The site of the state-run airline.
www.tourismthailand.org Official Thailand tourism site.

Recommended Hotels

Hotel prices vary widely across Phuket. Generally, the average hotel standard is more upmarket than elsewhere in Thailand, and the cost of a room is consequently higher than in Bangkok and on the other islands. The north of Phuket in particular has a lot of luxurious villas and upmarket accommodation.

The following price scale is based on high-season rack rates for a standard room per night, excluding the compulsory 7 percent VAT and 10 percent service charge. Prices can change dramatically from peak season (usually around 21 Dec–12 Jan) to low season, when a $$$ room may drop to $. If booking independently, always ask for discounts – most hotels will give them, particularly for longer stays. Even similar booking websites can vary greatly, as some are allotted promotional rates throughout the year by the hotels that favour them.

Prices rise substantially during the peak season. Most rooms are booked months in advance, so make a reservation early. Hotels often do renovations in the low season, so check that, too, to avoid unwanted noise.

$$$$$	over 8,000 baht
$$$$	6,000–8,000 baht
$$$	4,000–6,000 baht
$$	2,000–4,000 baht
$	below 2,000 baht

PATONG

Amari Coral Beach Resort Phuket $$ *Patong Beach; tel: 0 7634 0106-14; www.amari.com*. Perched on a headland at the quiet end of the beach, all rooms here have a private balcony and sea views. Three restaurants cover Thai, Italian and international foods, while the Si-vara Spa offers pampering treatments.

Avantika Boutique Hotel $$$ *41/1 Thaweewong Road; tel: 0 7629 2801-8; www.avantika-phuket.com*. This small and intimate beach-facing hotel has only 31 rooms. It's located opposite the beach at the quieter southern end of Patong, but with shops, bars and restaurants only a few minutes' walk away. The central Soi Bangla is approximately 10 minutes' walk away. Rooms are sophisticated in design, with dark woods offset against Thai silk furnishings, and all have ocean views. There's a swimming pool, spa, bar and restaurant.

Baan Yin Dee $$$$ *7/5 Meuan-Ngern Road; tel: 0 7629 4104-7; www. baanyindee.com.* A truly serene boutique resort with just 21 rooms and suites, all traditionally Thai in design, with dark woods, rattan furniture and white linens. Guest rooms, a terraced restaurant and an opulent four-tiered swimming pool all enjoy elevated sea views from a spectacular mountainside location.

Burasari $$$ *32/1 Ruamjai Road; tel: 0 7629 2929; www.burasari.com.* Burasari offers upmarket ambience at mid-range prices. The resort, on a quiet street set slightly back from the main beach road, has rooms positioned around the two central swimming pools, each surrounded by palms and tropical flowers. Shopping and dining amenities are nearby.

Expat Hotel $ *163/17 Rat Uthit Road; tel: 0 7634 2143; www.expathotel.com.* On the back road near the central street of Soi Bangla and a five-minute walk from the beach, the Expat Hotel is a favourite with return guests. Its old-style decor keeps prices lower than many other Patong hotels of similar standard. Clean rooms, friendly service and a large swimming pool make it great value for money.

Impiana Resort Patong $$$$ *41 Thaweewong Road; tel: 0 7634 2100; www.impiana.com.* Patong's only true beachfront accommodation. The luxuriously designed beach huts are on the sand and are well spaced to ensure privacy. Facilities within the main building reflect the indulgent nature of the resort, with a high-end spa and the exclusive Sala Bua restaurant, which is, again, Hat Patong's only true beachfront restaurant.

KARON

Andaman Seaview $$$$ *1 Karon Soi 4; tel: 0 7639 8111; www.andamanphuket.com.* Somewhat quirky in appearance, this place has white Corinthian-style pillars and different-coloured rooms on each of its four floors. A friendly, family-run establishment, it's is an excellent option for those wishing to avoid the carbon-copy type of chain hotel. Hat Karon is directly opposite, and Hat Kata is only a five-minute walk away. All rooms face the sea, and the 'deluxe pool access' rooms open directly onto a large swimming pool that winds around the hotel.

Hilton Phuket Arcadia Resort and Spa $$$ *333 Patak Road; tel: 0 7639 6433; www.hilton.com.* A huge and popular resort in the centre of Karon, with the beach a short walk away just across the road. Facilities include nine restaurants, five swimming pools, a spa, several tennis and squash courts, a playground, a putting green and free scuba diving lessons.

The Village Resort and Spa $$$$$ *566/1 Patak Road; tel: 0 7639 8200-5; www.thevillageresortandspa.com.* With only 34 artistic and somewhat eccentric-looking villas, each bearing an uncanny resemblance to the shape of a mushroom, this delightfully unique boutique resort appears to be hidden among jungle, yet is just opposite the beach. The quiet villas are split between pool view and jungle view, and are incredibly peaceful and romantic.

KATA

Aspasia $$$ *1/3 Laem Sai Road; tel: 0 7628 4430; www.aspasiaphuket. com.* An indulgent, Mediterranean-looking resort with mustard and terracotta walls offset with trailing vines and flowers. The bird's-eye sea views from the resort's elevated hillside position are fantastic. Rooms are modern and incredibly spacious. All have balconies and many have sunken jacuzzis in the bathrooms. A regular beach shuttle bus is available.

Kata Beach Resort and Spa $$$$$ *1 Pakbang Road; tel: 0 7633 0530-4; www.katagroup.com/katabeach.* Blessed with a prime position directly ahead of Kata Beach, this large yet relatively low-rise hotel projects a smaller, more intimate feel than its size would imply. Numerous facilities make it an excellent family choice, although couples will also benefit from an adults-only swimming pool and a romantic, dimly lit sea-facing restaurant.

Mom Tri's Boathouse Hotel $$$$$ *182 Koktanode Road; tel: 0 7633 0015-7; www.boathousephuket.com*. A very romantic boutique resort, which perfectly combines Western comforts with Eastern style. The peaceful ambience is heightened by the hotel's air of exclusivity, with an emphasis on intimate service and a relaxing and indulgent stay. There is direct beach access, and the sun sets over the sea, which all guest rooms face. Highly recommended for honeymooners.

Sugar Palm Resort and Spa $$$ *20/10 Kata Road; tel: 0 7628 4404; www.sugarpalmphuket.com*. A bright and modern hotel just a few minutes' stroll from Kata Beach and surrounded by a number of restaurants and small cafés. Spotlessly clean rooms are designed in soft cream with an individual accent colour, and all have balconies. A rectangular swimming pool with fountains and water features sits in the centre of this excellent-value hotel, which has frequent offers on room rates.

KAMALA

Aquamarine Resort and Spa $$$$ *17/36 Moo 6; tel: 0 7631 0600; www.aquamarineresort.com*. Dramatically perched upon the hilltop, this resort has dazzling sea views from all around, and from each of the Thai-designed rooms. It's very peaceful and tranquil due to its elevated position, but there's no beach access as a result. There is a regular shuttle bus, however, which makes the five-minute trip to nearby Hat Kamala throughout the day.

SURIN

Ayara Hilltops $$$$$ *125 Moo 3, Srisoonthorn Road; tel: 0 7627 1271; www.ayarahilltops.com*. Sea views are spectacular from the 48 villas comprising this striking boutique resort. Private suites are elevated on the mountainside, surrounded by palm trees, vines and flowers, and are well spaced along private walkways. The beach is within easy walking distance, and there is a sea-facing swimming pool. A number of rooms also have private outdoor swimming pools and/or jacuzzis.

The Surin Phuket $$$$$ *118 Moo 3, Choeng Thale; tel: 0 7662 1580; www.thesurinphuket.com.* Formerly The Chedi Resort and Spa, The Surin was redesigned in 2012 and now has a new beach bar and gym and the 103 cottages are now larger. Each has a sundeck facing the Andaman Sea. Some bungalows are on the sand, while others are at the resort's peak, from where views are fantastic, although a lot of walking is required. There is a striking octagonal black-tiled swimming pool, and one of Phuket's most upmarket spas on site.

BANG TAO

Amanpuri $$$$$ *118/1 Moo 3, Srisoonthorn Road; tel: 0 7632 4333; www.amanresorts.com.* Amanpuri is Phuket's most famous retreat, frequented predominantly by the rich and famous. It is unaffordable for many, but should your budget stretch this far you are guaranteed the ultimate in opulence and extravagance, from butler service in private villas to access to a fleet of luxury cruisers, which dock daily at the Amanpuri's private beach.

Banyan Tree Resort and Spa $$$$$ *33/7 Moo 4, Srisoonthorn Road; tel: 0 7632 4374; www.banyantree.com.* The most exclusive hotel in the Laguna Phuket group. The spacious villas have Thai-inspired decor and at least a private garden with sunken pool and jet pool. Some have swimming pools. There are additional pools on site, plus a golf course and golf school, tennis courts and a yoga teacher, among a host of facilities.

NAI YANG

Indigo Pearl $$$$$ *Nai Yang Beach and National Park; tel: 0 7632 7006; www.indigo-pearl.com.* There is beautiful design here in a wide range of suites, with lots of natural materials and interior styles ranging from funky to formal, traditional to modern. Some have private pools. Several dining options include Black Ginger, serving regional Southern Thai food in a traditional Thai building overlooking a lagoon.

MAI KHAO

JW Marriott Resort and Spa $$$$ *231 Moo 3, Mai Khao; tel: 0 7633 8000; www.marriott.com.* With an exclusive, secluded location as one of few hotels on Phuket's longest beach, this is ideal for those seeking to get away from it all. Consequently it's mainly suitable for a purely resort-based holiday. There are plenty of ways to fill your time, with lush tropical grounds, a top spa, beautiful infinity pool and activities from sailing to cooking classes.

PHUKET TOWN

On-On Hotel $ *19 Phang Nga Road; tel: 0 7621 1154.* Made famous by its role as the bustling backpacker hangout in the hit movie *The Beach*, this character-filled hotel is undeniably basic, but priced accordingly, with rooms starting at less than 200 baht a night. It's not overly comfortable for an extended stay, but an excellent budget place to meet other travellers and a good base from which to explore Phuket Town.

Royal Phuket City Hotel $$ *154 Phang Nga Road; tel: 0 7623 3333; www.royalphuketcity.com.* In the heart of town, this place has its own coffee shop and lounge area with a piano bar. It is Phuket Town's largest hotel, so slightly impersonal, but all sights are within walking distance, staff are friendly and rooms are clean and spacious.

LAEM PAN WA

Cape Panwa Hotel $$$ *27 Moo 8, Sakdidej Road; tel: 0 7639 1123; www.capepanwa.com.* Right on the beach, this stunning low-rise hotel is blessed with direct access to unspoilt sands, backed by rows of swaying palms. All rooms at Cape Panwa face the sea, and many of the newer rooms have jacuzzis and private pools. There are weekly cultural activities, including Thai cooking, Thai language lessons, Batik painting and massage classes.

Golden Tulip Mangosteen Resort and Spa $$$$ *99/4 Moo 7, Soi Mangosteen; tel: 0 7628 939; www.mangosteen-phuket.com*. An intimate resort with a sea view to one side and mountains to the other. Rooms have free Wi-fi, DVDs and flat-screen TVs and many have private jacuzzi baths. The saltwater swimming pool bends and twists its way around the resort's buildings and restaurant. There's no direct beach access, unfortunately; a shuttle bus is offered to Nai Harn beach and takes only five minutes.

The Royal Phuket Yacht Club $$$$$ *23/3 Moo 1, Viset Road; tel: 0 7638 0200; www.theroyalphuketyachtclub.com*. With direct access to Nai Harn beach, the Royal Phuket Yacht Club has the sparkling sea to its front and a lagoon at its back, and is in high demand year-round. Rooms, all with private terraces, are spacious and tastefully furnished. All have sea views, most overlooking the bay and nearby Promthep Cape. It's popular with those seeking a quiet beach away from the hustle and bustle further up the island.

KO HAE

Coral Island Resort $$ *48/11 Chaofa Road, Chalong Bay (postal address); tel: 0 7628 1060; www.coralislandresort.com*. This is the only accommodation on Coral Island, making it more highly priced than hotels of the equivalent standard on Phuket. It provides a comfortable stay, however, with clean, air-conditioned rooms and the only swimming pool on the island. It's quiet and very peaceful in the evenings once Phuket's day-trippers have left.

KO RACHA

The Racha $$$$$ *42/12–13 Moo 5, Rawai (postal address); tel: 0 7635 5455; www.theracha.com*. The perfect island getaway, accessible by private speedboat from mainland Phuket. Villas are decorated in elegant white, with garden bathrooms and rain showers. The rooftop infinity pool has uninterrupted sea views, and there is a luxurious spa and restaurant. It's a wonderful option for couples, but probably not suited to families with young children.

INDEX

Berlitz pocket guide

Phuket

Second Edition 2013

Written by Lauren Smith
Updated by Howard Richardson
Edited by Sian Lezard
Picture Researcher: Richard Cooke
Series Editor: Tom Stainer
Production: Tynan Dean, Linton Donaldson
and Rebeka Ellam

No part of this book may be reproduced, stored in a retrieval system or transmitted in any form or means electronic, mechanical, photocopying, recording or otherwise, without prior written permission from Berlitz Publishing. Brief text quotations with use of photographs are exempted for book review purposes only.

All Rights Reserved
© 2013 Apa Publications (UK) Limited

Printed in China by CTPS

Berlitz Trademark Reg. U.S. Patent Office and other countries. Marca Registrada. Used under licence from the Berlitz Investment Corporation

Photography credits: Anon 2ML; Corbis 22/23; David Henley/CPA 35; Fotolia 0/1, 2/3M, 4TL, 42, 59, 82, 89, 98/99; Ingolf Pompe 80; Joerg Kohler/Old Maps & Prints Co. Ltd 14/15; John Ishii/Apa Publications 2TL, 2TC, 2MC, 2/3T, 2/3M, 4ML, 4ML, 6TL, 6ML, 7MC, 7TC, 10, 11, 12, 14, 18, 20, 24, 26, 28, 36, 38/39, 40/41, 50, 52, 55, 56, 58, 60/61, 62, 64/65, 66, 73, 74, 75, 76/77, 78, 80/81, 83, 84, 90, 93, 94, 96, 100, 106; Marcus Wilson Smith/Apa Publications 16/17; Nakharin/Dreamstime.com 8; Nikt Wong/Apa Publications 3TC, 2/3M, 4TL, 4MR, 4/5M, 5MC, 4/5T, 5TC, 6ML, 7MC, 19, 21, 30, 31, 32/33, 34, 44, 45, 47, 48, 50/51, 52/53, 62/63, 68, 70, 72, 86, 103, 104
Cover picture: Alamy

Every effort has been made to provide accurate information in this publication, but changes are inevitable. The publisher cannot be responsible for any resulting loss, inconvenience or injury.

Contact us

At Berlitz we strive to keep our guides as accurate and up to date as possible, but if you find anything that has changed, or if you have any suggestions on ways to improve this guide, then we would be delighted to hear from you.

Berlitz Publishing, PO Box 7910,
London SE1 1WE, England.
email: berlitz@apaguide.co.uk
www.insightguides.com/berlitz